ASIAN IMMIGRANTS
IN "TWO CANADAS"

ASIAN IMMIGRANTS IN "TWO CANADAS"

Racialization, Marginalization, and Deregulated Work

HABIBA ZAMAN

Fernwood Publishing · Halifax & Winnipeg

Editing: Joyce Cameron
Cover design: John van der Woude
Printed and bound in Canada by Hignell Book Printing

Published in Canada by Fernwood Publishing
32 Oceanvista Lane, Black Point, Nova Scotia, B0J 1B0
and 748 Broadway Avenue, Winnipeg, Manitoba, R3G 0X3
www.fernwoodpublishing.ca

Fernwood Publishing Company Limited gratefully acknowledges the financial support of the Government of Canada through the Canada Book Fund and the Canada Council for the Arts, the Nova Scotia Department of Communities, Culture and Heritage, the Manitoba Department of Culture, Heritage and Tourism under the Manitoba Publishers Marketing Assistance Program and the Province of Manitoba, through the Book Publishing Tax Credit, for our publishing program.

Library and Archives Canada Cataloguing in Publication

Zaman, Habiba, 1950-
Asian immigrants in "Two Canadas": racialization,
marginalization and deregulated work / Habiba Zaman.

Includes bibliographical references.
ISBN 978-1-55266-479-7

1. Asian Canadians—Employment. 2. Immigrants—Canada—Employment.
3. Labor laws and legislation—Canada. 4. Asian Canadians—Economic conditions.
5. Asian Canadians—Social conditions. I. Title.

HD8108.5.A75Z35 2012   331.6'25071   C2011-908417-1

Contents

In memory of my compassionate and loving younger sister,
Sabera Khanam Nanni,
who adored me and was always proud of my academic work

Acknowledgements

This book owes its genesis to the report titled *Workplace Rights for Immigrants in BC: The Case of Filipino Workers* (both hard copy and online), which I did with my two co-authors, Cecilia Diocson and Rebecca Scott. The report was well received by academics, policy analysts, and local labour organizations, such as the Coalition for Employment Standards, as a step toward changing and improving the welfare of workers, particularly women under the Live-In Caregiver Program (LCP). The report, published in December 2007 by the Canadian Centre for Policy Alternatives (CCPA, British Columbia), was downloaded more than 6,400 times during the first four months in 2008 — one of the top BC downloads from the CCPA website. It was funded by a SSHRC-CURA grant (2004–2008) generally known as the Economic Security Project and a grant from the Vancouver Foundation.

My sincere gratitude and thanks to SSHRC-CURA and the Vancouver Foundation for the research grants, and to SSHRC-MCRI (2000–2005) and SSHRC/SFU Small Research (2008–2010) for the funds received for this study. Various kinds of assistance and support received from Simon Fraser University (SFU) Gender, Sexuality, and Women's Studies, Canadian Centre for Policy Alternatives, and the Philippine Women Centre in BC are also duly acknowledged. I would also like to take this opportunity to thank my research participants, without whom this book would not have been possible and whose help I would like to acknowledge here with gratitude. Many people — my co-researchers, research assistants, colleagues, students, administrators, staff, and friends — extended their encouragement and support to this book project. It is almost impossible to name them individually. Last but not the least, I would like to express my sincere gratitude and thanks to the following people: Cecilia Diocson, a co-researcher and internationally well-known Filipino community activist; Rebecca Scott, a research assistant who analyzed preliminary findings, formatted the tables, organized the workshop, and assisted me in navigating the intangible research route; Syeda Nayab Bukahri, who interviewed and transcribed some of the interviews; Rahela Nayebzadah, who helped me to understand the intricacies of the participants' narrations; and Suzanne Bastedo who provided assistance in sharpening my analysis.

This book manuscript was primarily written during my SFU sabbatical leave and Visiting Professorship in the Centre for Women's and Gender Studies/RAGA Centre at the University of British Columbia in 2010. My special thanks go to my publisher, Errol Sharpe, the editorial board of Fernwood Publishing, and the production team for their critical help in its completion.

My family has been a source of inspiration and support for me — always. My daughter Ayesha, my son Asif, my daughter-in-law Mubnii, and my life-long partner and long-time academic friend, Mohammad Zaman, have provided me with the emotional strength and support to complete this book. I am thankful to all of them.

Chapter 1

Introduction and Context

Migration has often been considered part of the solution for labour shortages and aging populations in OECD (Organization for Economic Cooperation and Development) countries. Canada is a member of the OECD and, like other OECD countries, relies on migrant labour to boost its demographic growth and address its labour shortages. As an immigrant-receiving country, Canada has a federally orchestrated Annual Immigration Plan, which every year brings more than a quarter of a million immigrants into Canada. The target in 2007 was to accept between 240,000 and 265,000 newcomers to fill Canada's "extraordinary" labour market requirements (*Globe and Mail*, November 1, 2006: A1).

Although Canada has four broad categories of immigrants — skilled (known as economic immigrants), business, family, and refugees — the skilled category (Editorial, *Geoforum*, 2005) has brought in more than 50 percent of immigrants since the beginning of the twenty-first century. Emphasis on the skilled category represents a dramatic shift from Canada's previous favouring of the family category and its historical demand for "unskilled" labour in the nineteenth century and the beginning of the twentieth. This emergence of the skilled category has occurred for a number of reasons: first, the advancement of digital technology and demand for specialized professions; second, the robust Canadian economy even in the global economic crisis of the first decade of the twenty-first century[1]; third, a shortage of professionals due to the fierce competition among industrialized countries to attract skilled labour; and finally, what Arat-Koç (1999) has identified as state restructuring of immigration policies due to neo-liberalism.

As a labour-recruiting tool, immigration policy has been devised in order to recruit skilled workers who are expected to help Canada advance to be economically competitive in the modern world economy. However, the International Labour Organization (ILO) sets global standards for employment, decent work, and economic security. Thus, one of the principal challenges for Canada in the twenty-first century is to ensure appropriate working conditions for all — including immigrants — to provide economic security, and to eliminate the traditional racialization and genderization of the labour market. It is widely documented that a racialized and genderized labour market in Canada has led to socio-political discontent and generally defeats the goals of a liberal democratic welfare state.[2] The general objective of this book is to examine how certain immigration and labour market policies and practices to date perpetuate segregated racialized

and genderized spaces and thus continue economic marginalization of Asian
immigrants in restructured work environments.

Historically, the labour market in Canada has been racialized and genderized,
as illustrated by the blatantly racist immigration policies that were in effect until
the 1960s (Jakubowski 1997). In the 1960s, Canada started to open its doors to
racialized people, although Europeans were allowed to sponsor broader categories
of relatives than racialized immigrants were (Taylor 1991). Finally, the *Immigration
Act* of 1976 removed racial discrimination and established a universal point system
regardless of racial or geographical origin. This point system prioritized education,
training, and occupational skills for selection and admission of immigrants. As a
result, Canada's demographic fabric in terms of race, ethnicity, birthplace, and
nationality of immigrants was gradually transformed (Halli and Driedger 1999).
Until 2002, the *Immigration Act* of 1976 guided Canadian immigration policies
and remained the principal legislation (Habib 2003). Further, the 1976 Act
actively encouraged family reunifications, and consequently, a larger number of
Asian immigrants gained entry under the family class category than through the
independent class (Simmons 1990; Thobani 1999). In 2001, the new *Immigration
and Refugee Protection Act* was introduced in Bill C-11 and came into effect on
June 28, 2002 (Habib 2003). Some of the positive changes included reducing
the sponsorship period from ten to three years and recognizing common-law and
same-sex couples for sponsorship. Important changes in the 2002 Act included
new selection criteria to attract more "highly skilled" and "adaptable" independent
immigrants.

The immigration acts of 1976 and 2002 thus facilitated a major demographic
shift in Canada from a non-racialized to a racialized immigrant population. Since
the last decade of the twentieth century, from six to seven of the top ten immigrant-
sending countries have been Asian countries.[3] These top source countries are
China, India, Pakistan, the Philippines, Korea, Sri Lanka, and Iran. By 2031, it is
predicted that one in three Canadians will belong to a racialized group while one
in four will be foreign-born, the highest proportion since the end of the last wave
of mass immigration, which began around 1910.[4] Currently, Canada maintains the
highest rate of immigration among OECD countries, largely from Asia.

It is considered that even a sudden decline of immigration would not
dramatically shift this demographic change, because racialized groups have the
higher birth rates and younger populations that Canada desperately needs. Further,
it is predicted that the demographic growth rate among racialized immigrant
groups will be higher in the next few decades compared to the rest of the Canadian
population. This prediction signals a large demographic change in the major
cities immigrants reside in, such as Toronto, Vancouver, and Montreal. Given
these trends, it is thought that racialized groups in major cities could account for
as much as 60 percent by 2031, which is only twenty years from now. In Metro
Vancouver, about 42 percent of people were classified as visible minorities in 2006.

By 2031, it is expected that the number will increase to 59 percent of the metro area population.[5] Based on these projections one can clearly see the rise of visible minority populations in major cities, and visible minorities will likely outnumber the demographically non-visible minority population within the foreseeable future. In other words, a visible minority majority[6] will emerge in the big cities by 2031. Out of the visible minorities, Asian immigrants will comprise the demographic majority in big cities. In the case of British Columbia (BC), Asian immigrants will emerge as a dominant and young labour pool due to the predominance of an already large Asian population in the city. Further, the geographical proximity of Asia and the location of more immigration offices in Asia (as compared with Africa, for example) may play a major role in Asian immigrants' predominance in BC. Several Asian countries where many speak English are in an advantageous position in terms of language[7] compared with Latin American countries. In the twenty-first century China and India, but particularly India where English is commonly spoken, have emerged as key players in the global economy, and their skilled workers continuously supply a young and vibrant labour pool to Canada.

Is this demographic shift to racialized groups in Canada reflected in the labour market, particularly in terms of Asian immigrants having decent work and economic security? Currently, there are no detailed in-depth studies on this issue. What is generally known is that most recent immigrants enter the labour market in flexible, temporary, non-standard, and economically insecure jobs (Grant and Sweetman 2004; Li 2001; Pictot 2004). As a result, a vast majority of "skilled" Asian immigrants who are mostly recent immigrants eventually transform into a "skilled proletariat" deprived of social security due to the restructuring of labour market policies and the nature of jobs they obtain. Does this racialized labour market reinforce the concept of "two Canadas,"[8] where racialized groups are concentrated in the lower echelons of the labour market? This apparent divisiveness in the workplace between racialized and non-racialized groups, where the concerns of one half have no resonance with the other, gives rise to two images of Canada in the labour market.[9] A key focus of this book is to explore this issue through survey responses and in-depth interviews of Asian immigrants in Greater Vancouver, and to document how the labour market policies and practices have led to the emergence of two Canadas within the Canadian welfare state.

The concept of "two Canadas" is problematic when one considers the Aboriginal population, i.e., the original inhabitants of Canada. One may incline towards extending the term to "three Canadas" in consideration of the racially exclusive white Canada nation-building project in the early inception of Canada as a state. The colonization and displacement of the indigenous population around the globe is a well-known fact and is lucidly documented in Roger Maaka and Chris Andersen's *The Indigenous Experience: Global Perspectives* (2006). In Canada, the displacement and colonization of the indigenous population was inextricably linked to early immigration, which eventually dispossessed the First Nations and resulted in the creation of reserve lands for them (Walker 2008). Recognizing the "two Canadas" concept as a contested and restricted category, this book demonstrates that "one Canada" concept is a myth when one considers the segregated/racialized space and economic insecurity for Asian immigrants in Canada. Since the focus of the book is on Asian immigrants only, the "two Canadas" concept is used to illustrate the labour market practices.

Canada has a prolonged political, economic, and social history of sustained and institutionalized racism.[10] For example, in the late 1800s and early 1900s, the Canadian state as well as an array of politicians from the national to the local level were influenced by groups like the Working Man's Protective Association, the Anti-Mongolian Association, and the Anti-Asiatic League, all formed to protect the English working class of BC from Asian immigrant workers, resulting in the *Chinese Exclusion Act*, in force from 1885 to 1947. The *Immigration Act* of 1885 imposed a tax of 50 dollars, commonly known as the "head tax," on all Chinese male labourers arriving in Canada. The tax rose to 500 dollars by 1903. To keep "Oriental aliens" out of Canada and to appease non-racialized groups, a number of stern measures were adopted, including deportation of all Asians who had not taken out citizenship, refusal of Asian burials in Christian cemeteries, and demolition of a disproportionate number of business buildings in Chinatown in Vancouver in the name of health and safety regulations. Without any alternate source of making a living many Chinese started small businesses. For these and many other Asians, the only other option was to work as domestic workers in non-racialized households.

In contrast to the nineteenth and most of the twentieth century, there are now apparently more options for most people wishing to immigrate to Canada. Many migrate to Canada not in the skilled category, but through other means, such as the family and business categories, the refugee program, a specialized category of domestic worker known as the Live-In Caregiver Program (LCP), or provincial government selection programs.[11] Li (2003: 4–5) explains why so many immigrants want to migrate to countries like Canada:

> [The] robustness of the highly developed economies also attracts others to venture to move, including those who are marginalized and displaced in their own countries as a result of economic globalization, capitalist expansion, and other social and political forces. For them, the advanced capitalist countries provide a chance to improve their livelihood, even though their lack of educational expertise and technical skills is likely to land them only in marginal sectors and in low-paying jobs. In short, in comparison to the harsh conditions, limited options, and growing uncertainty in their home countries, any slim chance of migrating to affluent countries is attractive, even it means working in menial jobs.

Although Canada's intake of categories of immigrants is comprehensive compared to most industrialized countries, it does not yet accept environmental refugees, i.e., refugees who have been displaced due to environmental disaster, such as the tsunami in Indonesia, the earthquake in Haiti, and so on. In the twenty-first century, with natural environment a major concern across the globe, it is still unknown how many people migrate to Canada due to environmental disaster. Despite the growing number of environmental refugees, an "environmental refugee" category is not yet recognized in immigration policy.

In Canada, immigration is largely a federal issue, while the workplace environment and labour are within provincial jurisdiction. The policies of the federal and provincial governments intersect with regard to the *Employment Standards Act* (ESA) as new immigrants enter the labour force. This book examines the interactions of selected federal and provincial policies and practices, and the implications of restructuring of the ESA in the workplace in view of the experience of Asian immigrants in the workplace and their basic economic security.

There are important reasons for consideration of these issues related to the labour market and workplace environments. First, achieving basic economic security through access to employment is considered an important aspect of social inclusion for immigrants, both in the workplace and in the wider society. So, how do basic economic security and social inclusion happen for Asian immigrants in the Canadian workplace? How do provincial government labour market regulations, and deregulations, provide or hinder security in the workplace? How does the federal government's current immigration policy naturalize social inequality in an already gendered and racialized labour market? Is basic economic security in the workplace still an illusion for Asian immigrants?

Using the ILO's comprehensive concept of basic economic security, this book explores the above questions as they pertain to Asian immigrants' labour market participation in Canada, more specifically in BC. This book investigates the ability of Asian immigrants to reasonably meet their economic security needs within the labour market. This province has experienced an economic boom in the past decade (2000–2010) compared to most provinces and is now more well known internationally for hosting the successful Winter Olympics in February 2010.

Conceptualizing Basic Economic Security

The ILO introduced basic security as a concept and as a central principle of ethical standpoint in its *Economic Security for a Better World* (2004). It names eight kinds of security fundamental to attaining economic security. These are: (i) basic security; (ii) labour market security; (iii) employment security; (iv) job security; (v) work security; (vi) skills security; (vii) income security; and (viii) representation and voice security. As can be seen in the ILO's list, work-related security is inherently tied to basic security. It is clear that while work-related security does not include everything the concept of security means, work-related security still plays an incredibly vital role. The ILO's report (2004: 3) contends that "real freedom cannot exist unless a certain level of economic security — basic security — exists." The

ILO report uses the concepts of basic and economic security interchangeably. This book uses the ILO approach to economic security. It should be mentioned that the ILO's report (2004) shies away from discussing discrimination based on "race", religion, sexual orientation, disability, transgender, and age — a significant limitation of the study.

The ILO characterizes security as freedom from debilitating risk, although not necessarily the freedom from all risk since risk-taking is considered necessary for individuals to develop and change. However, the ILO acknowledges that an overabundance of risk for any individual, group, business, or industry can have a debilitating rather than a beneficial effect. Risk, which the ILO characterizes as having a degree of predictability, can in excess quickly turn into insecurity, which has little predictability. Insecurity can have considerable costs, including financial, psychological, health, and social costs. In migrating to Canada, Asian immigrants take huge risks in terms of finding employment and having their professional skills and training recognized. In BC, there is mounting evidence that the risk and insecurity that immigrants bear has been accelerated by the deregulation of the province's ESA in 2002. This restructuring of BC's ESA will be examined in this book as an example of risk-transfer from more powerful individuals, businesses, and corporations, mostly dominated by non-racialized groups, to less powerful individuals, such as immigrant and racialized workers.

The federal government's immigration policy and the BC government's ESA are intertwined when it comes to racialized immigrants in the workplace. In this book, I argue that the basic security of Asian immigrants has been greatly compromised due to the deregulation of BC's ESA and the federal government's shift to the skilled category of immigrants. It is worth mentioning that the federal government has not formulated any standardized regulations for recognition of skills or for skill-transfer, even though immigration officers process applications based on skills. This book will argue that in order to reduce the period needed for immigrants to acquire economic security, it is absolutely essential for provincial policies to protect immigrant labourers' rights and keep them informed about their rights in the workplace.

Theoretical Framework

This book is guided by two major theoretical frameworks: political economy and spatial theory. The political economy approach pertinent to migration and immigration draws commonly on interdisciplinary studies which, at least for the purposes of this book, explore how the economics of immigrant/migrant labour, immigration law and policy, and the role of the provincial government in restructuring the ESA intersect in relation to Asian immigrants in Canada. In migration literature (Massey et al. 1993; Meyers 2000; Schiller & Basch 1995), the political economy approach views migration as serving the privileged class by keeping migrant labourers' wages down and eventually transforming these migrants into a reserve army for the continuous growth of capitalism. This approach argues that immigration counteracts the tendency of profits to fall and thus is a structural feature of capitalism and of the international division of labour.

One of the major drawbacks of the political economy approach is that its central thesis revolves around class while undermining race and gender. It generally deals with migration of labour across national borders/spaces rather than immigrant labour since immigration is considered a domestic issue located within a national boundary. Migrants and immigrants belong to two jurisdictional and social-entitlement spaces, although some migrants do become immigrants — for example, domestic workers in Canada under the LCP. In this book, the focal point is not migrants as conceptualized by political economy theory, but immigrants, including domestic workers,[12] whose country of origin/birthplace are in Asia.

The use of spatial theory in this book is influenced by Razack's edited book *Race, Space, and the Law: Unmapping a White Settler Society* (2002). Razack demonstrates that space is a socio-political-legal product that evolves gradually, orchestrated by city, provincial, and federal planners. Illustrating historical as well as contemporary specificities of space such as parks, slums, classrooms, urban spaces, provincial parliaments, and the location of mosques, the book explores how spaces are organized to sustain unequal and dialectical social relations between space and race, and thus produce and reproduce social hierarchies. However, despite the fact that spatial theory is a valuable tool for analyzing the dialectical relations between race and workplace, Razack's book does not include workplace as a "space."

Spatial theory guides this book in addressing an issue that has long been ignored in the literature: how has the workplace systematically and structurally produced and reproduced a racialized and genderized space for Asian immigrants, in this case in BC? The book argues that the BC provincial government's restructuring of the ESA has led to a racialized and genderized space perpetuating marginalization in the workplace and sustaining historical systemic and differential spaces in the workplace as well as in specific spaces like housing, neighbourhood, and transport.

Methodological Issues and Fieldwork Experience

The methodology of this study has been influenced by feminist and anti-racist frameworks (Agnew 2009; Razack 2002; Pratt 2004; Thobani 2007). Drawing on interdisciplinary texts and sources from sociology, anthropology, economics, political science, labour studies, geography, women's studies, and immigration and migration literature, the book will use a mix of quantitative and qualitative methods, although it relies more extensively on qualitative method.[13] The quantitative method employed is the analysis of Statistics Canada data, Citizenship and Immigration statistics, and a survey of one hundred Asian immigrants regarding their housing, transport, first job experience, place of residence, unemployment, and so on. The qualitative analysis encompasses in-depth interviews, focus and individual interviews, participation in various immigrant community and grassroots activities, and the conducting of a workshop attended by about sixty research participants, representatives from immigrant communities, and policy planners. In addition, content analysis of immigration literature and published and unpublished sources were used.

Interviews were conducted in three main ways: (i) a collaborative research project was undertaken with the Philippine Women Centre (PWC) in Vancouver under the guidance of Cecilia Diocson, who conducted a survey of one hundred participants and focus group participants as well as in-depth individual interviews with twenty-four Filipino immigrants; (ii) Syeda Nayab Bukhari, a Simon Fraser University PhD student in the Department of Gender, Sexuality, and Women's Studies, conducted twelve interviews with Pakistani immigrant women; and finally, (iii) I conducted thirteen individual interviews with immigrant women — ten from Bangladesh and three from India.

Cecilia, a seasoned researcher and an internationally known activist versatile in Tagalog and English, conducted interviews with Filipinos in both languages, depending upon the participant's choice of language. Retranslation, transcription, and editing of the interviews were performed under Cecilia's meticulous guidance, and thus the process can claim a high level of authenticity. Further, several volunteers of the PWC under Cecilia's supervision conducted the survey with the Filipino participants. Syeda, a Pakistani immigrant who can speak Pashtu, Urdu, Punjabi, and English, was an invaluable interviewer as the participants had diverse linguistic and ethnic backgrounds. Syeda greatly facilitated the location, selection, and even interviewing of these women, and she subsequently transcribed the interviews. Although I have been doing research with immigrants in BC for the past twelve years, not a single Pakistani woman had ever agreed to be interviewed for one of my projects until Syeda undertook this task in 2008. The Pakistani immigrant women's reluctance was primarily due to negative media coverage about Pakistani immigrants following 9/11 events in 2001 (see Zaman 2006).

The women I interviewed came mostly from my personal connections as well as from the India Mahila Association and the Greater Vancouver Bangladesh Cultural Association. Interviews were conducted in both Bangla and English, and it was the participant who selected the medium of language. Some participants were versatile in both Bangla and English (in the case of Bangladeshis) and some in Hindi, Punjabi, and English (in the case of those from India). Personal connections, the interviewer's fluency in the language of participants' countries of origin, and the snowball technique played a major role in locating participants, particularly in the case of Syeda. Syeda contacted immigrants from Pakistan in two immigrant settlement organizations who connected her to more skilled Pakistani women immigrants in Greater Vancouver.

Cecilia conducted most of the focus group interviews at the PWC, with very few individual interviews taking place at the participant's home. Cecilia works as a registered nurse in a major hospital, and she found it challenging to find a suitable time for the interviews. Most of the participants had on-call, part-time jobs and could not plan far ahead. For one focus group interview, for example, Cecilia set aside a Saturday off work, but received a phone call that most of the participants were unable to attend because they had been called in to work at the last minute. It was easier for me because I conducted interviews during the summer semester — a non-teaching, research semester — and that facilitated my accommodating most of the participants' schedules and need for last-minute cancellations.

All who conducted interviews were moved by the interview process, as we heard narratives revealing Asian immigrants' experiences in the workplace as well as in the wider society. It is worth noting that Syeda's interviewing experience with participants' husbands dispels the myth that Asian immigrant families invariably reflect an autocratic patriarchal structure. Syeda's experience resonates with mine interviewing people from Bangladesh and India. It seems that in many cases, the immigration process and settlement has the potential for reshaping, restructuring, and reinventing traditional gender roles.

One of the limitations of this study is that immigrants from China were not included. China is the foremost immigrant-sending country to Canada. However, financial constraints and lack of research personnel impeded my goal to interview immigrants from there. I hope that the research associated with this book will inspire other researchers to work with immigrants from China.

Although racism is pervasive in the workplace, the questionnaire used in the research for this book intentionally did not incorporate race or racism — the central enquiry concerned economic security and BC's ESA. Interestingly, the Asian immigrants' narratives indicated clearly that race, space, and gender intersect.

Contested Concepts

Some of the concepts used in this book are contested and carry an array of connotations, both negative and positive. These concepts thus require some explanation. For example, Statistics Canada uses the term "visible minority" as a demographic category connected with Canada's employment equity policies. The Canadian *Employment Equity Act* defines visible minorities as persons who are non-Caucasian in race or non-white in colour, and this definition excludes the First Nations. Employment equity programs frequently use the term "visible minority" to address labour market disadvantages of visible minorities. According to Boyd and Yiu (2009: 227), "Immigrant women are included in employment equity initiatives as women and, separately, as visible minorities. However, under the terms of the legislation, firms can comply with employment-equity requirements by hiring white women and visible minority men and by ignoring the foreign-born altogether." In other words, the *Employment Equity Act* is not proactive and may unwittingly create marginalized and segregated space for Asian immigrants, especially for Asian immigrant women. Further, the Canadian *Employment Equity Act's* definition of "visible minority" is Eurocentric: the reference point is "Caucasian" and "white."

The concept of visible minorities raises more controversy than consensus because it categorizes people based on skin colour, country of origin, and geographical location. Consequently, this book uses instead the concept of "racialization," which indicates a process that systematically and structurally discriminates and marginalizes certain groups based on the criteria of race. Agnew has eloquently elaborated on this concept in *Racialized Migrant Women in Canada: Essays on Health, Violence, and Equity* (2009). Distinguishing between the concepts of race and racialization, Agnew argues (2009: 8): "although race categorizes whites, racialization is a process that occurs in the context of power relations, whether it is in discourses, systemic to structures and institutions, or merely a matter of everyday encounters."

Another contested concept is "Asian immigrant." In this book, the concept refers to a geographical and continental location that unifies a racialized population as a political constituency in order to counter systemic and structural racism embedded in Canadian institutions. This notion is not an essentialist one, as it is grounded in Asian immigrants' individual and collective experience of institutional racism and marginalization and their resistance in myriad forms since the origin of the nation-state of Canada.

The narratives of diverse groups such as Bangladeshis, Indians, Filipinos, and Pakistanis clearly reflect their diversity in terms of religion (Islam, Christianity, Sikhism, Hinduism) and language (Tagalog, Bangla, Hindi, Punjabi, Urdu, Poshtu), nationality, ethnicity, and so on. However, participants are inextricably linked through their experience of the immigration process, landing the first job, employment in racialized spaces, and living in specific social spaces (East Vancouver, Surrey, Delta, etc.). Racialized spaces can be individual as well as collective. Individual racialized space refers to a racialized person's alienation and dislocation due to institutionalized racism. I agree that non-racialized people, for example single parents, people who live in poverty, gays, lesbians, and transgender people, also experience alienation and frustration; however, I argue that for immigrants, institutionalized racism has particularly far-reaching consequences including concentration in racialized spaces such as housing, neighbourhoods, workplaces, and so on.

The concept of the Asian immigrant has been extensively influenced by Mohanty's (1991: 7) exploration of "third world women":

> [A] viable oppositional alliance is a *common context of struggle* rather than color or racial identifications. Similarly, it is third world women's oppositional *political* relation to sexist, racist, and imperialist structures that constitutes our potential commonality. Thus, it is the common context of struggles against specific exploitative structures and systems that determines our potential political alliances.

The concept of "third world" is also much contested. For many, the term has negative connotations, appearing to promote the "first world" as ideal, progressive, modernized, and civilized. However, referring to contemporary and historical contexts, Mohanty uses "third world" as a unified political force with common grounds of resistance against oppressive forces, despite the term's divisiveness in terms of nationality, ethnicity, religions, etc. The use of Asian immigrants as a term thus functions as a catalyst unifying immigrants from countries in Asia. These immigrants can orchestrate resistance against institutional racism, whether it is the federal government's immigration policy or the provincial government's ESA, which accelerates deregulated work already pervasive in a racialized and genderized workplace. Further, the concept unifies Asian immigrants, whose specific ethnicity or nationality may provoke different allegiances and may produce stereotypes about a specific immigrant community. Ethnicity and nationality (i.e., country of origin) easily produce divisiveness. In addition, using the broad concept of the Asian immigrant provides more privacy and confidentiality to participants in citations of their testimonies in the text. For example, a Bangladeshi immigrant's story may be identified by another Bangladeshi immigrant because the community is still not very large and interacts closely at various events, such as picnics, the celebration of Tagore's 150th anniversary, Independence Day and Mother Language Day.

Literature on Immigrants: Issues and Limitations

As Canada is a country of immigrants, literature on immigrants is vast and reflects diverse academic interests. Broadly, immigration literature is divided into four comprehensive categories, although they intersect in myriad forms: (i) demographic (Halli and Driedger 1999; Li 2003); (ii) anti-racist (Calliste and Dei 2000; Dossa 2009; Thobani 2007; Walker 2008); (iii) policy-oriented (*Canadian Issues* 2003, 2005, 2008; *Canadian Diversity* 2008); and (iv) labour studies (Gupta 2009; Stasiulis and Bakan 2005). This immigration literature generally deals with content and discourse analysis, uses census data and Statistics Canada's surveys on immigrants, and includes historical review of immigration materials. A good amount of literature deals with migrant workers' rights and focuses on Mexican farm workers, Filipino domestic workers, seasonal workers, and so on (Basok 2003; Giles and Arat-Koç 1994; Stasiulis and Bakan 2005). The use of immigrants' narratives to analyze immigrants' workplaces generally, let alone to analyze Asian immigrants' workplaces, is almost non-existent, although some labour studies literature does focus on immigrants (Vosko 2006) and some anti-racist literature focuses on racism in the workplace (Gupta 2009). Labour studies scholarship recognizes racialized immigrant workers' marginalization but does not treat immigrant workers' voices separately. In a nutshell, immigration literature has hardly begun to describe racialized immigrants' experiences in the workplace. In contrast, this book aims to reveal Asian immigrants' experiences in the workplace through their own voices.

This book makes recent Asian immigrants its major focus. Citizenship and Immigration Canada (CIC) uses "very recent" or "most recent" to describe those immigrants who arrived within the past five years, while "recent" immigrants includes those who arrived within the past fifteen years (Infometrica: ix). In this book, in order to examine the effect of BC's restructuring of its ESA in 2002, I use the concept of "recent immigrants" to refer only to those who arrived in the past five years. In addition, immigrants who came to Canada more than five years ago were interviewed to demonstrate racialization, marginalization in the workplace, and individual as well as collective agency in the wider society.

Structure of the Book

The ILO's array of concepts pertinent to basic/economic security and the restructuring of the ESA in BC will be examined next, in Chapter Two. Chapter Three will report on the results of a survey of one hundred recent Filipino immigrants and provides a comprehensive overview of Asian immigrants' housing, transport, neighbourhood/geographical space, types of jobs, employment and unemployment, patterns of settlement, nature of racism experienced, participation in the labour market and experience in the workplace environment, and the role of religion in their lives. Chapter Four will examine individual immigrants' testimonies illustrating job security, employment security, skills security, income security, and voice and representation security, as well as overall basic economic security. These accounts reveal how spaces have been reproduced, allocated, and relocated for Asian immigrants. Through an array of immigrants' interview testimonies Chapter Five will explore work security that enhances or jeopardizes the workplace environment. Chapter Six will illustrate how Asian immigrants exert their individual and collective agency in the workplace and at the same time long for social benefits and economic security. Based on a workshop and the research findings, this chapter will recommend alternative policies. Chapter Seven will summarize the contributions of the book.

Notes

1. Canada's dollar was almost at par with the US dollar in 2008 and 2009 and remained so even in 2010, when economic recession hit hard globally, including in the US. The surging price of housing in most parts of Canada is one of the indicators of a robust economy. Indeed, many parts of the world consider Canada a role model for economic growth and financial stability, especially in the banking sectors.
2. Esping–Anderson (1990) has classified three broad typologies of welfare state regimes: liberal, conservative, and social democratic. Liberal regimes foster market provisions of services. Examples include Canada, Australia, Great Britain, and the United States. However, variations in the domestic arena occur among these countries' social policies.
3. Out of the top ten immigrant-sending countries, the number of Asian countries has continuously been six or seven in the list since the beginning of the twenty-first century—a dramatic increase from the twentieth century.
4. Joe Friesen (*Globe and Mail,* March 10, 2010: A1) has reported that one in three

Canadians will be a visible minority by 2031 and this change could lead to "divisions and cultural clashes."

5. Miro Cernetig (*Vancouver Sun*, March 10, 2010: A1) reported that by 2031, 59 percent of the population of Vancouver will be visible minorities.

6. The concept "minority-majority" has been very much influenced by Maria Lourdes Carrillo's term "majority world" encompassing both migrants and immigrants, although the inclusion of indigenous/aborigine population may not happen in these kinds of "non-aboriginal projects." For details, see pages 9–10 in Carrillo's thesis "Socially Transformative Transnational Feminism: Filipino Women Activists at Home and Abroad" (unpublished PhD dissertation, University of British Columbia, 2009).

7. English and French are the two official languages in Canada. Immigration officials give preference to people who can speak one of these official languages, provided other factors remain equal.

8. "Two Canadas" is a metaphor often used throughout Canada's history. Recently, it was used by the director of the Maytree Foundation and cited in a widely publicized *Globe and Mail* (March 10, 2010: A9) article that expressed the fact that Canada is divided along race lines despite the existence of multiculturalism policy and basic welfare policies. The existence of two Canadas will be demonstrated throughout this book through the quotation of first-person narratives.

9. The formation of the nation-state and the inception of the settler society that produced systemic and institutionalized racism against indigenous populations in Canada are beyond the purview of this book. This book focuses on a racialized group originating from a specific geographical entity, Asia, which is the principal source of immigrant-sending countries to Canada in the twenty-first century. Other racialized immigrant groups, such as people of African or Latin American descent, are not included in this analysis.

10. Daphne Bramham (*Vancouver* Sun, April 3, 2010: A5) reported that as part of a reconciliation process, the city of New Westminister is the first Canadian city that has admitted its "sustained and institutionalized racism against Chinese." She also mentioned the dark history of Canada, which made it "almost impossible for Chinese to earn a living there unless they were servants."

11. Quebec selects its own immigrants, and criteria for immigrants to Quebec differ from the criteria of the federal government. To fill their provincial labour market needs, British Columbia, Manitoba, Saskatchewan, and New Brunswick have agreements with the federal government regarding the selection of provincial nominees. Although provincial nominees do not have to meet the federal selection criteria, they must pass health and security requirements.

12. Once they apply, almost 99 percent of domestic workers achieve immigrant status after meeting the immigration requirements, i.e., working in a Canadian household as a domestic worker for twenty-four months within a three-year period. The current Annual Immigration Plan of Canada has a quota of 4,000 for domestic workers.

13. The research for this book project received funds from several sources including a SSHRC-MCRI grant (2000–2005), a SSHC-CURA grant (2004–2008), the Vancouver Foundation (2006–2007), and an SFU/SSHRC Small Research Grant (2008–2009). In addition, SFU Financial Services Work-Study projects (2000–2009) supported several undergraduate and graduate students in collecting secondary materials.

Chapter 2

Economic Security, Decent Work,
BC's Employment Standards Act, and Restructuring

With its comprehensive work, *Economic Security for a Better World* (2004), the International Labour Organization (ILO) has developed the most significant study available on the concept of economic security. The ILO study reflects a global focus and, more specifically, a focus on "third-world"[1] countries. But how does economic security play out in a developed country such as Canada?

In BC, insecurity for immigrants became more systemic and chronic as a result of the *Employment Standards Act*'s deregulation in the name of restructuring labour rights and because of the lack of provincial government monitoring in the workplace. In fact, because it takes a lengthy period for recent immigrants to acquire economic security, their interim labour market experience may become a liability rather than an asset as their unskilled employment can detract from the appearance of their work records on their résumés.

In Canada, employment standards legislation — the legislation providing basic protections for workers in the labour market — is an individual province's domain. In 2001, the provincial government in BC restructured economic and labour market policies, including the ESA, and the social service sectors, including housing and welfare (for details, see Fairey 2005; Irwin, McBride and Strubin 2005; Wallace, Klein and Reitsma-Street 2006). The changes to the ESA have had profound impacts on the labour market experience of Asian immigrants. In brief, these amendments reduced the enforcement role of the government, removed protections for workers, reduced employment-related benefits, and slashed the minimum wage for first-time workers, including recent immigrants. Indeed, the restructuring had the effect of making working conditions unregulated. The resulting lack of monitoring of wages and conditions in workplaces profoundly affects the ability of recent Asian immigrants to find economic security and decent work within the labour market.

What exactly is decent work? Most people expect that it is work suitable for the worker, adequately paid, personally safe, free of harassment, and so on. At the beginning of the twenty-first century, the International Labour Organization introduced a new concept, decent work, indicating "an environment of basic economic security" (ILO 2004: 275).[2] This book uses the concept of decent work pertinent to the ILO's seven kinds of economic security (as listed in Chapter One). Standing (2004) calls "decent work" a vision for the twenty-first century. Using the vision of decent work,[3] this book and its accompanying research examine how the ILO's robust concept of economic security relates to the BC labour market and Asian immigrants in BC in the current neo-liberal context.

The ILO's Array of Concepts Pertinent to Economic Security

The ILO argues (2004: 9): "Most low-income individuals, households, families and communities face what might be called systemic insecurity, or chronic, rather than stochastic (or what is sometimes called 'idiosyncratic') insecurity. In other words, one or more 'shocks' can easily jeopardize their capacity to function effectively." Low-income individuals and families devote a great deal of time to risk management and are often at the brink of the shocks that they can manage. Certainly, this is especially true of recent immigrants to Canada in their first few years after arrival, whatever the category in which they entered.

The ILO (2004: 3) points out that increasing unrest throughout the world is the result of the shifting of risk from groups like government and businesses onto individuals, especially those with low incomes: "In recent decades, and apparently stretching into the future, it seems that ordinary workers and working communities — and societies on the edge of the capitalist economy — are being obliged to bear most of the worst forms of insecurity, whereas large-scale asset-holders are relatively well shielded from insecurity." This neo-liberal trend is clearly identifiable in the changes to the *Employment Standards Act* being discussed in this chapter.

In light of the BC Liberal government's restructuring of the ESA in 2002, Standing's (2004: 3) notion of security in *Promoting Income Security as a Right* is instructive: "A key point about 'security' is that whatever is provided must be assured. There is no 'moving of the goal posts,' which has been a striking feature of most welfare states over the past fifty years." According to Sanding, the notion of economic security needs to be expanded — economic security must not be thought of as only the "social safety net" that performs risk compensation. Standing (2004: 13) argues: "ask not what social protection must protect you *against*; ask what social protection can protect you *for*." This means developing policies and programs that enhance individuals' and groups' power to develop. Considered in this light, BC has a long way to move towards economic security.

As introduced in Chapter One, this book uses the term "economic security" as comprehensively as possible, referring to the seven kinds of basic economic security outlined by the ILO: (1) labour market security, (2) employment security, (3) job security, (4) work security, (5) skills security, (6) income security, and (7) representation and voice security.

The ILO (2004: 5) states that basic security means "limiting the uncertainties people face in their daily lives ... providing a social environment in which people ... feel they belong to a range of communities, and have a fair and good opportunity to live a decent life and [to acquire] ... decent work." According to Standing, basic security includes equality of freedom and protection against morbidity, and only economic and social security can ensure true freedom — the freedom to develop. Standing (2004: 2–4) further elaborates that this basic kind of security constitutes an individual's ability to develop capacities and to live purposefully and rationally, i.e., free from paternalism, debilitating fear, or debilitating risk management. Basic security provides a fair opportunity to acquire a decent life, including decent work and decent accommodation. While both the ILO's and Standing's definitions of basic security extend beyond the scope of this book, it is clear that the concepts of basic security and decent work are inextricably linked; thus they are used interchangeably throughout this book.

Labour Market Security

Labour market security refers to the presence of adequate employment opportunities, i.e., not expecting workers to rely on part-time, temporary, informal, and non-standard employment. Labour market security is compromised by the informalization of the labour market and the proliferation of non-standard work in opposition to standard work that is full-time, permanent, full-year employment, with a single employer. In general, part-time, temporary, flexible, and informal workers do not receive any benefits, significantly reducing employers' costs. These non-standard jobs compromise workers' access to benefits that would enhance their economic security. Moreover, in these jobs weekly hours of work are considered flexible, and a company utilizes employees' labour only when needed. The International Labour Organization (2004: 115) characterizes such jobs as having "a lack of social protection, lack of regulatory safeguards, and general precariousness."

Employment Security

Employment security includes protection mechanisms against wrongful or arbitrary dismissal and against loss of income from work. The factors impacting employment security are: 1) employment tenure: workers with long tenure are more likely to have higher employment security; 2) the size of the firm: smaller firms are more likely to go out of business, leading to job loss; and 3) employment contracts: protections are frequently entrenched in contracts or collective agreements. The ILO points out recent trends include weakened legislation, structural changes, and the consequences that arise from employment insecurity. In fact, structural changes have eroded employment security. In order to increase labour market flexibility, the ILO argues, governments have introduced several changes in laws and regulations that eventually erode employment protection. The ILO is critical of the trend towards flexibilization, as this seems to be the trend most threatening to employment security.

Job Security

Job security refers to the control a worker has over the content of a job that assists the worker in building a career. Job security cannot be found in a job where the kind and quantity of tasks are undesirable and stagnant, with little room for mobility. Job security differs from employment security: employment security is characterized by an attachment to a particular place of work, while job security is characterized by an attachment to an array of tasks.

The ILO finds that three factors have an impact on workers' job security: 1) the ability to retain one job without being arbitrarily transferred to another; 2) the ability to have options in a job situation where the tasks have become obsolete; and 3) the ability to challenge discrimination or institutional barriers to work opportunities that include mobility. The ILO argues that because anti-discrimination policies prescribe equal opportunities, they may be a major barrier to job security. According to the ILO, anti-discrimination policies may create three kinds of discrimination that affect job security: 1) categorical discrimination against visibly identifiable groups (for example, Asian immigrants); 2) statistical discrimination (for example, Canada's Employment Equity category, "visible minority," which can lead to excluding racialized women); and 3) inferential discrimination, which can arise when viewing an application from a prospective employee (for example, Oreopoulos' report [2009] points out that job applicants with English names have a much better chance of getting an interview than those with Chinese, Indian, or Pakistani names). The ILO (2004: 223) relates its findings mostly to discrimination against women, finding that in every country studied, "discriminatory practices against women are more common in small firms and greater in private than in public (state) firms." It can also be said with some confidence that a woman's job security can be compromised by pregnancy.

Work Security

Work security refers to working conditions promoting a worker's well-being and safety. Thus, work security includes occupational health and safety as well as mental and emotional well-being. The ILO's index for measuring work security uses indicators such as laws on occupational health and safety, government expenditure on compensation, the existence of safety committees, and work-related injury and fatality rates.

Regarding labour market restructuring, the ILO finds that downsizing and the increased use of temporary and casual labour, as well as outsourcing (contracting work to sources outside the company), cause greater work insecurity. Structural change decreases work security. The ILO also introduces the concept of time security, arguing that the poor spend more time on activities that do not generate income, but do relate to work — for example, travelling to work by bus. Time security will be explored further in Chapter Three in the survey findings and in Chapter Four in Asian immigrants' interview testimonies.

Experiences of work security are profoundly unequal as awareness of workplace hazards and mechanisms for remedying hazards vary among groups of workers. For example, some groups, such as women, immigrants, and youth, are more likely to work in an unsafe work environment and less likely to have protection or compensation for injury or workplace violations by the employer. Further, women more often than men encounter various forms of harassment, including sexual harassment, in the workplace.

Skills Security

The various elements of skills security as outlined by the International Labour Organization are as follows: 1) access to schooling, measured by the level of schooling attained; 2) access to training beyond school, which includes vocational training; 3) utilization of training; 4) perceived adequacy of skills; 5) perceived need for training; and 6) ability to use a computer. Utilization of training and perceived adequacy of skills are particularly relevant for the study associated with this book since participants in the survey experienced high levels of de-skilling, underemployment, and unemployment, and most believed that they were overqualified for the jobs they performed in Canada. Unfortunately, although there is an obvious link, the ILO does not relate skill utilization to immigration.

The ILO links skills security to the other forms of security, and three factors raised are especially pertinent to this study: 1) more schooling is positively linked to higher income; 2) employment security is positively linked to access to training; and 3) there is a positive correlation between voice and representation security and skills security. However, the ILO does not explore the important relation between wages and access to training, which emerges in the survey and in-depth interviews reported in this book.

Income Security

Income security is perhaps the most important and immediate form of economic security. According to the ILO (2004: 55), income security is "an adequate level of income, a reasonable assurance that such an income will continue, a sense that the income is fair, relative to actual and perceived 'needs' and relative to the income of others, and the assurance of compensation or support in the eventuality of a shock or crisis affecting income." Income includes payment for work in the form of wages and salaries, but can also include many other things, such as employer-provided benefits (medical, dental, subsidized transportation, etc.) and benefits such as remittances. "Public goods," which can include universal health care and policing, are also considered to be part of one's income because if they are not provided by the state, they must be paid for by individuals.

Representation and Voice Security

In terms of economic security, the ILO (2004: 247) notes that "voice is required for many purposes in the sphere of work, the most notable being to negotiate over wages, benefits and working conditions. It is also needed for monitoring working practices, for information-gathering, and for evaluating the impact of work practices or policies." In this way, security is constituted not only in the opportunity and ability to speak but also in the opportunity to be heard. Here, Asian immigrants have a special case in at least three ways. First, Asian immigrants often have a language barrier that prevents them from fully expressing themselves in the dominant language and may silence them altogether. English as a Second Language (ESL) programs become of utmost importance to those Asian immigrants who cannot communicate effectively in the dominant language. Second, due to racism and discrimination, some Asian immigrants' voices are ignored, discouraged, or suppressed, and this can lead to internalized silence. Finally, since Asian immigrants, and particularly Asian immigrant women, tend to be concentrated in the low-wage service sector, voice representation — in the form of unions, for example — is often denied.

Representation and voice security is important for economic security because it constitutes the ability of individuals or groups — in this study, Asian immigrants — to advance their own interests, needs, and rights. Without this kind of security, exploitation is much more likely to occur. Standing (2004: 12) finds that "any agenda that sees the extension of rights or freedoms without collective *representation security* [Standing's emphasis] could mean only that the vulnerable would remain vulnerable."

The Restructuring of the ESA in BC

Asian immigrants are one of the groups in BC which has historically experienced more economic insecurity than non-racialized groups. The changes to BC's *Employment Standards Act* (ESA) may have made Asian immigrants even more susceptible to debilitating shocks to their livelihood. This section examines the ESA, which historically protected vulnerable workers, including Asian immigrants, and indicates how changes to the ESA can profoundly affect Asian immigrants' experience in the labour market.

The ESA was originally introduced in BC to provide employees with minimum standards for every workplace that falls under provincial jurisdiction. The ideology of such an act was clear: if left to market forces, employees would suffer from poor workplace conditions, especially vulnerable employees such as young workers, women, and immigrants. The implication was that if employers could be trusted to handle employee affairs in a fair and equitable manner, there would be no need for such an act. In other words, the fundamental purpose of the ESA was to provide minimum rights and standards that might not otherwise be provided for workers due to the intrinsic power imbalance between workers and employers. The ESA could also function to enhance human rights, such as the freedom from discrimination. By its very nature, the ESA's purpose is to protect the most vulnerable, including women, youth, and racialized groups, including — most relevant to this study — Asian immigrants.

In 2001, the BC government began a process of sweeping employment standards reform. Major changes were made to the Act and its regulations, and numerous regulatory amendments were passed. The changes to the ESA were the topic of much discussion and critique in the media and among several activist groups. Critical perspectives came from several online news sources[4] in addition to print sources. The Canadian Centre for Policy Alternatives (CCPA) in BC took a prominent lead in critiquing the restructuring of BC's ESA (Fairey 2002 and 2005; Fudge 2005; Fuller 2004; Klein 2002; MacDonald 2002). However, outside of the CCPA, there have been no substantive critical studies of an academic nature on the impact of the 2002 restructuring of the ESA, and there has been little on the impact of the ESA as it relates to racialized immigrants, including Asian immigrants.[5] This book and its associated study seek to address this gap.

In May 2002, the BC government introduced major changes to its labour market policies, which set out minimum standards incorporating workplace rights in areas such as hours of work, minimum wages, termination, statutory holidays, overtime, and vacation time. Historically, labour market policies protected non-union workers and guided unions and employers to set numerous minimum standards in negotiating a collective agreement. In general, the BC government's 2002 major amendments to its labour market policies shifted power in favour of employers and removed "restrictions" on them, allowing them to make work schedules "flexible" in a way that eventually benefits employers. The amendments reduced the role of government in implementing labour market policies, and the government reduced administration and protection activities it had carried out previously. Restructuring the regulations as well as making the regulations more "flexible" has had far-reaching consequences for one of the province's most disadvantaged and vulnerable groups: Asian immigrants. The following is an overview of certain changes to the ESA in 2002 and a discussion of their impact on racialized immigrants, recent immigrants, and immigrant women, and more specifically on Asian immigrants.

At the time of writing, the notorious "training wage" of the 2002 Act has been repealed and the minimum wage has finally been raised — long-awaited responses to popular demand. However, other aspects of the Act that were introduced in 2002 remain unchanged and continue to serve employers to the detriment of workers, particularly the most vulnerable workers, amongst them Asian immigrants. In either case — whether the government has yielded to public pressure or continues to maintain the parts of the Act that were amended in 2002 to shift power further towards employers — it is important to analyze the role and impact of neo-liberal legislation and policy changes on immigrant populations and to understand the potential of collective agency.

Daily Minimum Hours

Prior to the changes to the ESA, employees were entitled to a minimum of four hours pay if they showed up for scheduled or on-call work but were sent home for any reason, except under conditions completely beyond the employer's control. (One example of a condition beyond the employer's control is bad weather, in which case the employee was paid for two hours.) This provision took into consideration that employees plan their expenses around expected wages and incur travel costs in getting to work. With the changes to the ESA, the minimum was reduced to two hours, unless the employee had been scheduled for more than eight hours that day, in which case the employee would be entitled to be paid for four hours.

The change of the daily minimum hours clearly leaves employees more vulnerable to unpredictability in the workplace. It constitutes a forced flexibility as the employee's potential to earn wages is now more affected by the fluctuations of the workplace and marketplace. The liability for these fluctuations has shifted away from companies and onto employees, forcing them to be "flexible" so that employers do not have to be. Furthermore, this change affects those with non-standard employment more than those with standard, formalized employment. The precarious nature of part-time work is thus exacerbated by this change. The provincial government claimed that this change would create "new employment opportunities" for workers; in fact, this change has removed barriers to employers so that they can call in employees when required even for two hours, which absolutely ignores a worker's travel time to work. A two-hour on-call day is hardly a decent opportunity or decent work for any worker.

Training Wage

The minimum wage in BC remained at eight dollars per hour from 2001 until 2011. As well, in 2002 the government introduced a "training wage" of six dollars per hour, which remained in place until May of 2011. With the training wage, employers were legally entitled to pay "inexperienced" workers six dollars an hour for up to five hundred work hours. After five hundred hours, employers were to begin paying the minimum wage, i.e., eight dollars per hour. Working in other provinces or countries was supposed to count as hours of experience, but it was difficult for many workers to provide the necessary documentation to prove their work experience. The policy impetus of the training wage was supposedly to increase youth employment. However, anyone without the minimum hours, such as mothers entering the workforce for the first time, or immigrants or refugees without sufficient documentation of paid work in countries of origin (not considering translation), could be paid a training wage. Furthermore, the survey discussed in the following chapters included a participant who received the training wage even after five hundred hours of employment in Canada, clearly a contravention of the Act.

Once employees reached five hundred hours of employment, no enforcement mechanisms existed to ensure they were not fired and replaced with other inexperienced or vulnerable workers, such as recent immigrants, again paid at the training wage. While not legally permitted to fire employees for reaching the five hundred hours, employers can, at their discretion, dismiss employees at any time. Thus, employees who received the training wage may have had difficulty holding their jobs after five hundred hours. Moreover, the added burden of having been terminated from a previous job, which almost every prospective employer would frown upon, put dismissed employees at a competitive disadvantage compared to other "inexperienced" workers. In sum, the training wage provides a disincentive to providing employment security for young, inexperienced, or vulnerable workers, including new immigrants. Furthermore, the government neither gathered statistics on the pervasiveness of the training wage nor intervened in workplaces that paid it. Employees were expected to self-report any violations!

A clear contradiction existed in the training wage. Many workers who received the training wage reported they did not receive any training, and the survey associated with this book affirms this. A fair wage would have the opposite effect and would encourage training, as the Canadian Labour Congress (CLC) (2005: 37) asserts: "The fact that employers are under pressure to pay good wages will lead them to invest more in capital equipment and in training than would otherwise be the case." It is clear that increasing, not decreasing, the minimum wage gives employers the incentive to train their workers. The training wage affirmed that racialized immigrants' labour is cheap and disposable. This wage was so unpopular that on March 16, 2011, two days after assuming office, Premier Christie Clarke announced the repeal of the training wage category.[6]

Overtime

With the 2002 changes to the *Employment Standards Act*, every employee covered by the Act and all those professions governed by special regulations had their overtime entitlement lessened. Generally, the amount of overtime an employee must work to be entitled to double time increased from eleven to twelve hours. In addition, the entitlement to weekly double overtime pay was repealed. This means employees work more or the same amount of overtime at a lower cost to the employer. Thus, productivity/output per wage dollar increased to the benefit of employers but at the expense of employees.

Statutory Holidays

Previously under the ESA, every employee was entitled to statutory holiday pay. If employees worked on a statutory holiday, they were entitled to a day off with pay in addition to statutory holiday pay of time-and-a-half. As a result of the changes to the ESA, only employees who have worked fifteen of the thirty calendar days previous to a statutory holiday are entitled to statutory pay. Consequently, if an employee was sick or otherwise unable to work fifteen of the past thirty days, their statutory pay is compromised. Further, employers are no longer required to give employees who work a statutory holiday a day off in lieu of the statutory holiday. The impact of these changes is greatest on part-time workers who have the most "flexible" work schedules. Anyone working less than four days a week would rarely, if ever, meet the fifteen-day requirement. These are other examples of how employees working part-time have seen their real wages decrease due to changes to the ESA, and the impact is similar to the ones associated with changes in minimum hours.

Averaging Agreements

The 2002 ESA introduced averaging agreements to replace flexible work schedules. Prior to the changes, 65 percent of affected employees had to agree on flexible work schedules. This requirement meant that some sort of collective discussion took place and facilitated the possibility for employees to act as a group, discussing the proposed schedule and informing each other of its benefits and drawbacks. Thus, employees could, in theory, act in a unified fashion in negotiating a mutually beneficial schedule. In addition, the director of the Employment Standards Branch would be provided with a copy of the schedule as an interventionist measure to ensure that it complied with the Act, as well as documentation proving that 65 percent of the employees had agreed.

With the changes to the ESA, the unified nature of negotiations has been removed. The schedules are now negotiated and agreed upon on an individual basis. Since there is no longer encouragement to discuss with other employees the benefits and drawbacks of schedules or to share knowledge of the specifications of the Act (which are, in fact, quite complex), the employee is more vulnerable to pressure to sign an unfair agreement. Employers have considerable power over employees, for example the power to fire and to deny advancement or raises. So, while it may seem that individuals are empowered to negotiate a schedule that is best for them, it is likely that the employer's interests will prevail over the employees. Thus, averaging agreements can compromise employees' sense of employment security, encouraging them to be more "flexible," which actually means less protected from the changing and forceful nature of the marketplace. This trend towards individualization is in line with many of the other changes in the Act. For example, the individualized nature of schedule negotiation is similar to the individualized approach to conflict resolution that the Ministry has taken with the introduction of the "Self-Help Kit." These are both examples of how neo-liberal "self-reliance" works in practice.

Posting of Workers' Rights Eliminated

A major change made to the Act was the removal of the requirement to post workers' rights in the workplace. Posting this information was probably very easy to comply with and benefited employees, especially immigrants and first-time employees, who might not otherwise be fully informed of their rights. Now that workers' rights are no longer posted, employees are more susceptible to exploitation.

"Self-Help Kit"

The introduction of the "Self-Help Kit" for employees not covered by a collective agreement is the change to the resolution process that probably most affects the individual worker. Using the kit is the required first step that employees must take if they have a grievance with their employer, and the first of a few changes to the Act showing the non-interventionist attitude of the government towards upholding employment standards. Using the "Self-Help Kit," called a guide for dispute resolution, requires both a level of knowledge of employment standards and a certain degree of literacy. As discussed in the previous section, the removal of the requirement to post information on workers' rights means that many workers will no longer be aware of their rights or the employment standards. Further, language barriers are likely to prevent many Asian immigrant workers from successfully receiving protection or wage recovery through the "Self-Help Kit," as the ESA is lengthy and complicated. Even though legally entitled to wages or protection, employees may give up fighting a matter and focus only on their most serious complaints. Or, employees may be completely unaware of certain rights. If an employee does not feel comfortable discussing issues with the employer, the Employment Standards Branch may dismiss the complaint because the employee did not use the kit. Another problem with the kit is that it assumes that employers have mechanisms in place for dealing with complaints and are familiar with the provisions of the Act. The kit is simply a clumsy and confusing bureaucratic barrier designed to discourage workers from the "costly" procedure of demanding their rights.

Settlement Agreements

The 2002 changes to the Act gave settlement agreements a new formal status. With the previous Act, a settlement agreement between two parties, such as an employee and their employer, was not binding if one of the parties failed to comply. In such cases, the settlement agreement would then be deemed void. The director of the Employment Standards Branch would be required to investigate the matter and make an independent determination, which could result in one party having to pay more to the other party than was originally required by the settlement agreement.

With the changes to the ESA, settlement agreements are considered binding and cannot be voided by the director of the Employment Standards Branch. Thus, it is in the employer's best interest to come up with a settlement agreement rather than be subject to a full investigation, which could uncover more liability. Employees in a hurry to recover at least some of their wages may be pressed to sign a settlement agreement that awards them less than they truly deserve under the Act. Again, employees and employers are encouraged to settle their own matters without intervention by the Employment Standards Branch, whose ultimate role seems to be to intervene as little as possible, and the arrangement works to the disadvantage of employees.

Investigation

The wording of the Act has changed from "the director must investigate a complaint made," to "the director must accept and review a complaint made." This means that the director can use discretion about investigating a complaint, and some complaints that previously would have to have been investigated will now be left unexplored. In other words, "review a complaint made" is not the same as "investigate a complaint made." In this way also, the government is taking a lax approach to upholding employment standards.

Wage Liability/ Record-Keeping

With the changes to the ESA, employers are now liable for far less wages than they were before. The amount of wages that an employee can recover has been greatly reduced from twenty-four months to six months. This means that an employee has only six months to file a complaint for wages owed, and wages that became payable six months ago or more cannot be recovered under the Act. Long-standing wage contravention thus has a severely reduced penalty. In addition, the length of time for which the Employment Standards Branch can demand to see payroll records has been reduced from five years to two years. This means that, for example, in the case of vacation pay, which is based on prior years worked, the employer does not have to show the records that may be needed to pursue the complaint.

Penalties

The government heralded its changes to the penalty schedule as "cracking down" on those who have repeatedly contravened the Act. Changes include making penalties mandatory, as well as making them escalating depending on whether the employer has repeatedly contravened the Act. The previous penalty schedule was zero dollars for a first offence, $150 for a second, $250 for a third, and $500 for each subsequent contravention, with each amount being multiplied by the number of employees affected. The new schedule is as follows: $500 for a first contravention, $2,500 for a second, and $10,000 for a third.

Unfortunately, the appearance of greater punishment for repeat offenders is an illusion. Under the previous Act, an escalating penalty could be imposed for contravening a provision that was in the same part of the Act as the first contravention. However, the new regulations specify that an escalating penalty is given only if the same specific provision of the Act is contravened within a three-year period. This means that exactly the same contravention must occur three times for a penalty to reach $10,000, and contraventions that occurred more than three years ago do not result in an escalated penalty. The escalating penalties are also illusory because the revised Act removed the requirement for the Employment Standards Branch to investigate complaints. That, along with the requirement that employees begin the process using the "Self-Help Kit," means that fewer determinations will be made, and thus fewer penalties issued. As a result of these changes, employers are likely to have less fear of being penalized and therefore may be less motivated to adhere to the standards in the Act.

The new penalties are larger, but this again is an illusion since the penalties are no longer multiplied by the number of employees affected. For example, five hundred dollars is hardly a penalty for a contravention that affects hundreds of employees. The only way for a penalty to be a significant disincentive to contravention is to make the penalty more expensive than the amount an employer saves by contravening the Act. These new penalty amounts are still too low to prevent harm to workers.

Another change in the ESA regarding penalties is that the period of time that payroll records must be kept is now much shorter than before. It is now two years, whereas previously it was five. It is evident that some employers do not keep accurate records of employment, making it difficult for participants to prove their claims to wages, Employment Insurance benefits, etc. But instead of rectifying this problem, the government changed the Act to allow employers to keep records for far less time. This means that workers' ability to prove violations of the Act and receive compensation is often doubly compromised. The government either completely ignored or did not investigate the reality of record keeping when it changed the Act in this way.

Complaint Procedures/Investigation

Under the 2002 changes to the *Employment Standards Act* (ESA), grievance procedures are largely complaints-based. According to the Canadian Labour Congress (2005: 29), the flaw of the system is that a lack of complaints does not necessarily mean compliance; non-compliance can be "just as high in firms from which no complaints have been filed as in firms from which complaints originated."

Not only are investigation procedures complaints-based, but the director has discretion about which complaints will be investigated, as pointed out in an earlier section. According to the CLC (2005: 28), this situation continues under the changed Act despite the fact that "proactive inspections ... [have] success in uncovering violations." Further, prior to the 2002 Act, employees who were covered by a collective agreement could rely on the Employment Standards Branch to override the agreement if it stipulated working conditions and wages below those in the *Employment Standards Act*. This is no longer the case. With the changes to the Act, the ESB now has no jurisdiction to intervene in virtually any workplace where employees are covered by a collective agreement.

Conclusion

The changes to BC's ESA and its regulations show a major shift in the government's role in implementing and upholding employment standards. The trend towards individualization and self-reliance is most clearly demonstrated by the introduction of averaging agreements and the implementation of the "Self-Help Kit." The trend towards devolution of authority for upholding standards is shown through the new formal status of settlement agreements and, in the case of unionized workplaces, the fact that the ESB can no longer enforce the conditions of the *Employment Standards Act* as a minimum in collective agreements. Finally, the trend towards lowering standards for employees to the benefit of employers is shown by the decrease in overtime entitlement as well as in the reduction in minimum hours. It seems that the ultimate goal of these changes is to reduce the size and power of the Employment Standards Branch. A lesser role for government is an obvious neo-liberal strategy, which, this chapter has shown, leaves employees vulnerable to the dynamics of the competitive economy, and can create major repercussions for employees' quality of life, i.e., their economic security.

Restructuring in the ESA reflects a shift in favour of corporations and laissez-faire economics, inevitably leading to economic insecurity and an inhospitable work environment for Asian immigrants in BC. This restructuring of labour market policies encompasses both deregulation and decentralization and has shifted the province's policies to the ideology of flexibility. The changes to the ESA, the legislation that provides basic protection for workers in the workplace, have had profound impacts on the labour market experience of Asian immigrants. These amendments reduced the enforcement role of the government, removed protection for workers, reduced employment-related benefits, and slashed the minimum wage for first-time workers, including recent immigrants, who are mostly Asians. Indeed, the changes make working conditions unregulated and clearly indicate the provincial Liberal government's continuous shift towards those who are privileged and powerful.

Many factors constitute the dimensions of security for individuals and groups. In order to get a comprehensive picture of the situation for Asian immigrants, a survey was undertaken to assess issues such as Asian immigrants' access to housing, child care, transportation, first job experience, place of residence, and unemployment. Chapter Three will use the survey results to comprehensively examine economic security, considering these various forms as they pertain to the general situation of Asian immigrants and especially immigrant women in the BC labour market.

Notes

1. As mentioned in Chapter One, the concepts "third world" and "first world" as used here have been influenced by Mohanty's (1991) political categorization.
2. Acknowledging the role of the ILO in promoting decent work for both women and men, Ghai (2006) has provided a comprehensive analytical framework to the concept and substance of decent work. However, Ghai's treatment of decent work in a general, global way weakens its usefulness in a Canadian context, i.e., what is decent work in Canada? Egger and Sengenberger (2003: xi) offer the following definition of decent work: "Decent work stems from the convergence of four strategic objectives, namely the promotion of rights at work; employment; social protections; and social dialogue." However, Egger and Sengenberger focus entirely on Denmark, a very different country from Canada, with dissimilar challenges. These works by Ghai and Egger and Sengenberger have provided this book with a base from which to develop a Canadian-specific concept.
3. There is no consensus on economic security and decent work across countries, despite the ILO's report, as the concepts vary from first world to third world. Further, the concepts vary among first-world countries if one considers Esping-Anderson's

typologies. Esping-Anderson (1990) classified three broad typologies of welfare state: liberal, conservative, and social-democratic. According to this typology, Canada is a liberal welfare state and Denmark is a social-democratic welfare state.

4.   These studies are: *Info for Change* (which includes fact sheets on new employment legislation and discussion of the repercussions of those changes), at <infoforchange. bc.ca>; 2) *The People's Law School: Working in BC: Your Legal Rights and Responsibilities* (provides legal information on a variety of topics), at <publiclegaled.bc.ca/working/>; and 3) *6 Bucks Sucks* (for young people to get information and share ideas about the training wage), at <6buckssucks.com/>.

5.   One exception is a study by Moore (2004) on seasonal farm workers, mostly migrants and recent immigrants, and the restructuring of the ESA. This study is largely drawn from Indo-Canadian community members who are mostly middle-aged and older, and have lived in the Lower Mainland in BC for less than five years.

6.   Clarke also raised the minimum hourly wage on a staggered basis: from $8.00 to $8.75 on May 1, 2011; $9.50 on November 1, 2011; and $10.25 on May 1, 2012.

Chapter 3

Recent Immigrants

An Example of Racialized and Marginalized Space

Filipino immigrants were selected as the sample group for the survey for this study because this community has many characteristics particularly relevant in terms of the economic security of immigrants. The collaborative project with the Philippine Women Centre (PWC) in Vancouver facilitated the survey being conducted across BC. Cecilia Diocson, who conducted the survey with the one hundred individual and focus group participants, is a seasoned researcher and an internationally known activist versatile in Tagalong and English. She also supervised several volunteers of the Philippine Women Centre who conducted the survey.

Although racism is pervasive in the workplace, the questionnaire used in the research for this book intentionally did not incorporate race or racism — the central enquiry concerned economic security and BC's *Employment Standards Act*. Interestingly, the Asian immigrants' narratives indicated clearly that race, space, and gender intersect. The survey findings and overall trends are not unique to this group; policy implications, including restructuring of the ESA and its impacts upon Filipino immigrants, can be extended to many racialized immigrants, particularly those from Asia.

Although a significantly large and vocal racialized community across Canada, Filipinos are a quite recent arrivals. Between July 2003 and June 2004, the number of immigrants from the Philippines rose 56 percent over the same period in the previous year (Citizenship and Immigration Canada *The Monitor* Fall 2004). In both 2002 and 2003, when changes to the ESA occurred, the Philippines ranked fourth among top source countries for principal applicants and their dependants (CIC *The Monitor* Spring 2004). Filipinos are predominantly recent immigrants to Canada (Kelly 2006), and this makes them an ideal group for a focused sample study pertinent to recent immigrants.

This chapter outlines the Live-in Caregiver Program (LCP) and Filipino immigration to Canada, then presents the survey findings in two ways: first, a demographic profile of the participants, and second, their experiences of various levels of security in the BC labour market. All names used are pseudonyms chosen by the participants.

The LCP and Filipino Immigration to Canada

The context of Filipino immigration to Canada is the Philippines' aggressive labour export policy combined with a skills shortage in Canada and the economy-oriented policies of Citizenship and Immigration Canada. To reduce high unemployment levels and to recover from a stagnant economy through continuous remittance (money sent home) from migrant workers, the Philippines aggressively promotes a labour export policy. Consequently, thousands of migrant workers leave the country daily. At the same time, Canadian policy has focused overtly on the economics of immigration and the need for a cheap labour pool. Consequently, Canada's immigration policy is dominated by solutions to the labour market's immediate needs, and workers' basic security is compromised in multiple dimensions. A speech to the Standing Committee on Citizenship and Immigration in 2005 by the Minister of Citizenship and Immigration reflects this approach to immigration policy: "We're also working very hard to find ways that we can make the immigration program more responsive to labour market needs" (CIC 2005b).

One outcome of the combination of Canadian immigration policy and the Philippines' labour export policy is an influx of Filipino immigrants to Canada as live-in caregivers. Canada has experienced a significant labour shortage of live-in caregivers because the government provides inadequate support for child care and other programs requiring caregivers. The goal of the Live-in Caregiver Program is to bring qualified workers to perform live-in work because Canadians are unavailable to fill the positions (CIC 2005a). The LCP exists due to the shortage of Canadians or permanent residents to fill the need for live-in caregiving work.

Live-in caregivers as migrant workers must live in their employer's home and provide services for children, the elderly, or the disabled. After twenty-four months of employment as a live-in caregiver within three years at the time of the survey, but as of April 2010 within four years, the caregiver is entitled to apply for permanent residency/immigrant status — labelled among caregivers as "open visa." These immigrants are required to work only as live-in caregivers until they attain permanent status, and then for the time required in order to process immigration papers.

Not all Filipino immigrants migrate to Canada as live-in caregivers, as is evidenced by the diverse profile of participants in the survey as well as by the fact that thirty-seven of the one hundred Filipino immigrants surveyed came into Canada in either the skilled workers category or as dependants of Filipino immigrants. However, the majority of participants in this survey are or were live-in caregivers. Several studies (Bakan and Stasiulis 1994, 1997; England and Stiell 1997; Pratt 1999; Zaman 2004) have suggested that the Philippines is the major supplier for LCP participants in Canada. More than half of Filipino immigrants in the economic category — of which the LCP is considered a part — are either live-in caregivers or their dependants. The vast majority of live-in caregivers are women, which indicates that the LCP policies are also feminized, i.e., the policies create a gendered pattern of employment. In fact, 59 percent of the increase in Filipino immigrants mentioned above is comprised of women (CIC 2004a).

It is worth exploring the LCP as it relates to economic security, racialized immigrants, the Philippines, and the BC government's restructuring of labour policies in the beginning of the twenty-first century. Sharma (2001: 423) argues that migrants, or temporary workers, in this case LCP workers, "are made to work in unfree employment relationships as a condition of entering, residing and working in Canada." While not all temporary workers in Canada should be considered "unfree wage workers" — for example, foreign students working on temporary visas — migrants working in certain sectors, such as in the LCP, have stipulations placed on their employment. These can include what kind of work they may do, where they may reside — for example, that they must live in their employer's home — and what programs and benefits they have access to in Canada. These stipulations, according to Sharma (2001), create both systemic and legislated disempowerment designed to remove political, economic, labour, and social rights and, ultimately, to create a highly flexible, cheap labour force. This structural disempowerment during the first phase of migration initiates and perpetuates a racialized and marginalized space for Asian immigrants, in this case, the LCP workers.

Most Filipino caregivers are highly skilled, the majority with degrees from the Philippines, and several in the survey were in nursing or teaching positions in their country of origin. However, almost all live-in caregivers in Canada receive extremely low wages after deductions for room and board. This exploitative situation is often justified with what is seen as a fair trade-off for a poor wage and inhospitable working conditions: the ability to eventually apply for permanent residency and citizenship. As Pratt (2003: 4) argues, "The 'wrong' of Canadians taking such obvious advantage of economic misery elsewhere is set 'right' by bestowing permanent residency on those who function responsibly within the LCP." The question then arises: What happens to live-in caregivers after they obtain permanent residency? The answer, according to the research associated with this book, is that they continue to experience a range of insecurities and are forced to navigate in racialized and marginalized spaces in many sectors including housing, transportation, job seeking, and inhospitable work environments. These findings support Pratt's study (2003: 2), which found that after seven years, "Most women [had] experience[d] long-term downward occupational mobility and continue[d] to do domestic work as housekeepers and home care health workers." These women's inability to be upwardly mobile is due to the gendered and racialized space allocated for domestic labour, which is supported by neo-liberal policies regarding child care, skills security, and education.

As was discussed in Chapter Two, another factor contributing to downward mobility arises from 2002 changes to the *Employment Standards Act*. Furthermore, the fact that many migrant workers are expected to remit a portion of their earnings to support family members in the Philippines can prevent them from focusing or spending money on their own education or upgrading (Pratt 2003: 11). In other words, immigration policies, changes to the ESA, and the demands of domestic work create real barriers to employment mobility and security for these women and make them economically insecure in a designated racialized domain, i.e., all kinds of caregiving ranging from child care to elder care to disabled care. Economic insecurity, racialized and gendered space, the LCP in Canada, and changes to the ESA intersect in complex and systemic ways.

The high level of education of Filipino immigrants and their relative lack of labour mobility or ability to find gainful employment in their professions in Canada make them an ideal group to study in terms of exploring skills security and employment security. The federal government often hails immigration policy as addressing labour market needs and skills shortages within the skilled worker program. However, the evidence suggests that it is not always skilled workers that are needed in the labour market. Both the survey and the associated interviews showed that new immigrants can get work fairly quickly, but in the low-wage service sector that is generally identified as "unskilled." Most immigrants in the survey found that if they tried to enter the professions for which they were trained, obtaining recognition of their credentials involved one confusing barrier after another. Despite the Citizenship and Immigration Canada's policies to attract skilled workers, it is clear that immigrants experience skills insecurity. As pointed out in Chapter Two, skills insecurity and employment insecurity are relevant to economic security because they prevent immigrants from integrating fully into the labour market and from obtaining job security and income security.

Filipino immigrants are an extremely active and politicized group in Canada, especially in Vancouver. They organize protests and demonstrations to make their collective voices heard both at the provincial and federal levels, as will be discussed in Chapter Six. In terms of policy alternatives, this community takes a proactive role in developing strategies to meet their needs and push policy makers to listen and adopt these strategies. For example, the PWC, in consultation with the Filipino community, published a report, *Enhancing Capability and Visibility: Filipinas in Public Policy Engagement* (Diocson 2005), which includes a list of policy recommendations. The vibrancy that comes from this kind of empowerment in the midst of economic insecurity is important to immigrants. For me, engaging with the FWC and its community in a partnership initiative to develop viable policy alternatives to eliminate racialized and gendered space is a step towards enacting socio-economic-political change in the present.

Survey Findings: Demographic Profile

This section presents a demographic profile of the one hundred Filipinos who participated in the survey. The profile includes immigration categories, years of arrival, educational attainment, basic security, work experience in country of origin and other countries, reasons for immigrating, places of residence, kinds of housing, use of transportation, child care, remittance, and access to education in Canada. The survey findings are complemented by excerpts from the in-depth interviews with Asian immigrants.

Immigration Categories

Citizenship and Immigration, as we have seen earlier, admits immigrants into Canada under various categories. Currently, the most predominant is the skilled category, often called the economic category, which includes independent immigrants. As Table 1 shows, caregivers are overrepresented in the survey, comprising 67 percent of the sample. This overrepresentation is due to three factors. First, Filipinos make up the majority of caregivers due

Table 1: Categories of Immigration

Category	Number
Domestic worker	67
Family category	20
Independent immigrant	7
Spouse	6
Business category	0
Refugee	0
Other	0
Total	100

to Canadian immigration policy and the Philippines' aggressive labour export policy. Second, PWC, the community collaborator, selected the participants for the survey from immigrants who had made contact with the centre either to seek help or to become members. As has been argued by many scholars (Bakan and Stasiulis 1997; Pratt 1999; Zaman 2006), caregivers are among the most marginalized of immigrant workers and are more likely to seek community support in dealing with the employers with whom they live. Third, since caregivers experience many forms of marginalization, including racialization at a heightened level, they are particularly relevant to discussions of economic security and deregulation of the ESA. Interestingly, there were no refugees in the survey, indicating that these Filipinos emigrated more for economic than for political reasons.

Years of Arrival

This sample was primarily made up of recent immigrants, but it also included a few immigrants who had been in Canada for a long time, making a comparison of their experiences possible. As can be seen in Table 2, the majority of participants were either recent immigrants (twenty-five participants who had lived in Canada ten or fewer years) or very recent immigrants (fifty-five participants who had lived in Canada for fewer than five years).

Table 2: Number of Participants According to Year of Arrival

Years of Arrival	Number
Prior to 1990	8
1990 to 1994	12
1995 to 1999	25
2000-2005	55
Total	100

Table 2 supports the Citizenship and Immigration Canada data discussed earlier, showing that immigration from the Philippines is on the rise in the twenty-first century. Table 2 also reflects the cycles of the Canadian economy, showing the connection between immigration and the economy, i.e., the recessions of the 1980s and early 1990s and the resulting lower intake of immigrants.

Educational Attainment

Since the attainment of education among the one hundred survey participants was very high — for example, fifty-six have an undergraduate degree — this study's findings endorse a growing body of literature critical of the lack of credential recognition, the process of re-skilling, and training programs in Canada (Reitz 2001; Zaman 2006).[1] Rosa, one of the survey participants, succinctly identifies skills security as a central issue for Filipino

Table 3: Educational Attainment in the Philippines

Level of Education	Number
Above undergraduate	2
Undergraduate	56
Some college/university	4
Trade/vocational	10
No post-secondary	28
Total	100

immigrants: "We don't need programs. We need and want the Canadian government to recognize our education." As Table 3 shows, more than half the participants had at least an undergraduate degree. The most common undergraduate degree was in nursing: twenty-one participants reported having received a nursing degree in the Philippines. Three participants had a degree in education and four in commerce. Other degrees included mathematics, pharmacology, agricultural economics, psychology, and architecture. Besides degrees, many participants had other kinds of training. For example, several of the participants with vocational training were trained midwives.

Of the twenty-eight participants who reported not obtaining any post-secondary education in the Philippines, many had migrated when they were younger than working age. Seventeen participants reported undertaking some form of post-secondary education in Canada. Of these seventeen, eleven completed the education. The actual levels of education attained by all the participants were thus even higher, with eighty-three of the one hundred participants having some form of post-secondary education.

Basic Security

In terms of basic security, a number of participants reported a gap between their expectations for life in Canada and their actual experience. The following is a selection of responses to the question, "What was your expectation of Canadian life?":

> Oasis: To find a job related to my training and education.
> Bebot: To work as a health worker.
> Emmie: [It would be] easy to get a job, and you can use your

educational background.
Mary: [I was] expecting [that] Canada has lots of opportunity.

When they migrated to Canada, many participants hoped to work in the profession for which they were trained. However, their first jobs in Canada and the kinds of jobs these participants worked in at the time of the survey showed that their hopes had mostly gone unfulfilled. In Canada, the participants were very unlikely to obtain work in a profession related to their training; they also experienced very little upward occupational mobility, as evidenced by their current jobs. The systemic barriers that prevent these trained people from working in their professions eventually led them to become a racialized and marginalized workforce with access only to lower echelons of the job market. It is becoming evident that the increasing concentration of racialized individuals in the low-wage sectors is creating a specific space designated, however unwittingly, for a certain group based on race.

Work Experience in Country of Origin and other Countries

Although it was common to migrate directly after the completion of education, many participants in the survey had work experience in their trained professions in the Philippines. The lack of job opportunities in the Philippines, combined with a belief in the opportunities in Canada, motivated many participants to immigrate. In the Philippines, some participants had entry-level jobs, working, for example, as salespeople and cashiers, but most had professional jobs such as nursing and teaching. Several reported working for the Philippine government.

Besides having work experience in the Philippines, some participants also worked in other countries in the professions for which they were trained. It is clear that some participants' skills were in demand elsewhere. For example, Noble and Gracy worked in Singapore, Memy in Taiwan, and Jillian in Saudi Arabia. All of these women worked as nurses before they came to Canada but became caregivers once they reached this country. Nelia, who worked as a nurse in Libya, Saudi Arabia, and Sudan, talked about the demand for her skills:

> You know about Filipino nurses. Once they go to other countries and [are] given recognition, they are really good nurses. Our skills are really tops.... We have good educational and professional records. And we are ready to compete. We thought that we could do this in Canada because this is what we had been doing — competing with others in terms of our skills and knowledge.

However, the most common job for Filipinas abroad was caregiving. Hong Kong was the most common destination, with fourteen participants having worked there. Another nine had worked in Singapore. The Middle East was also a common destination, with some participants having worked in Dubai, Yemen, and Saudi Arabia. While this study cannot answer the question, a further study could find out whether the families for whom caregivers work in Hong Kong and the Middle East are Americans or Canadians or other non-locals (e.g., embassies and international organizations) and whether the genderized and racialized relations of care-giving in Canada and the United States extend into these geographical areas.

Reasons for Immigrating

Most of the immigrants surveyed had very high expectations of what Canada would be like, especially regarding economic security and labour market conditions. The majority of participants reported that they immigrated for largely economic reasons. Sixty-eight participants reported that obtaining a job in Canada was one of their top three reasons for immigrating to Canada. Of these, thirty rated obtaining a job as their number one reason. Twenty-three participants named poverty as a reason for immigrating, providing evidence of the economic push-and-pull factors involved in migration.

Family reasons were also a major factor. Forty-eight participants reported that family was a top-three reason for immigration; of those, forty-five cited family as the most important reason. It is possible that some participants immigrated for family reunification, while others immigrated in order to provide remittance for family members in the Philippines, a practice very common among this study's participants.

Thirty-one participants reported that their children's education was a top-three reason for immigrating — a further emphasis on the family. Only nineteen participants reported their own higher education as a reason for immigrating. This finding can be attributed to the fact that this group was already highly educated and had work experience in their country of origin. Interestingly, just seven participants reported political uncertainty as a reason for migrating.

Most participants hoped for positive changes in their lives when they made the decision to immigrate to Canada. Seeking "adventure" and "a better future" were common sentiments stated. Hope for a "better life" was expressed by several participants, who noted that they expected the political and economic conditions to be better in Canada and looked forward to medical benefits, health care, and a higher standard of living. The following are some responses to the question, "What was your expectation of Canadian life?":

> Ron: [An] improved life.
> Kreskne: It's going to be easy and more liberated compared to that third-world country.
> Noble: [Canada has a] very high standard of living.
> Aurean: Canada would give me and my family a better life.
> Inday: [Canada has] socialized medical, health care.
> Rubia: Freedom attained and comforts.
> Memy: [Canada has] better living conditions [and a] low cost of living.

Many participants expressed romanticized notions of what Canada would be like. The following are other responses to the same question.

> Kikay: Green pasture land.
> Mar: Land of milk and honey — great expectation[s].
> Rambo: Paradise.
> Bing: Peaceful and greener pastures.
> Julia: For better or greener pastures.
> Clara: I heard that Canada is very good and [has] freedom.

Places of Residence

According to Citizenship and Immigration Canada, Filipino immigrants are more likely than other immigrants to settle outside the major metropolitan areas of Montreal, Toronto, and Vancouver. In 2004, 38 percent of Filipino immigrants were settling in areas outside these cities compared with just 28 percent of other immigrant arrivals (CIC 2004a). This statistic may well reflect the need for live-in caregivers in smaller cities or rural areas.

Where survey participants lived — in urban centres, small cities, and rural areas — revealed a cross-section

Table 4: Number of Participants Residing in Specific Areas of Vancouver

Residential Location	Number
Downtown Eastside	33
Vancouver (West, South, etc.)	16
Kelowna	9
Surrey	9
Richmond/Delta	8
New Westminster, Coquitlam, Burnaby	8
Victoria	2
Others (not mentioned)	15
Total	100

of experiences. The majority of participants resided in municipalities throughout southern BC, with most concentrated in the Greater Vancouver Regional District and some living in Victoria and Kelowna. It was possible to include participants from various places in BC because the Philippine Women Centre has either contacts or centres in these regions.

The most common place of residence for the participants was the Downtown Eastside (DES) in Vancouver. This is probably not a coincidence because there is a large Filipino community in the DES, and both the PWC and the Kalayaan Centre — a centre for all Filipinos — are located there. Any Filipinos living in this area likely have contact with the Kalayaan Centre. In terms of areas of residence in Greater Vancouver, the DES is well known as an area populated with people from a cross-section of society including sex workers, drug users, new and racialized immigrants, and the homeless. The residents are from a wide range of incomes, including very low incomes. These factors along with the presence of the PWC, the Kalayaan Centre, and other Filipinos made the Downtown Eastside a common area of residence among the participants.

While job diversity existed among participants from other areas, the majority of participants who lived in Kelowna worked or used to work as caregivers. As mentioned earlier, perhaps there is high demand for live-in caregivers in this smaller city as well as in rural areas due to the unavailability of child-care centres.

Kinds of Housing

The majority of participants rented their accommodation. This included twenty who rented apartments, sixteen who rented basement suites, fifteen who rented detached houses, four who rented duplexes, and three who rented townhouses. Only eleven participants owned their accommodation: two owned their apartments and nine owned a detached house. The remaining thirty-one participants lived in their employers' homes.

No participants lived alone. On average, there were four or five individuals living in each dwelling. Since this number included those who lived in apartments or basement suites, these participants may have experienced overcrowding. Indeed, some participants complained that their dwellings were too small. No participant paid more than $1,000 in housing charges (mortgage or rent) per month; most paid from $700 to $800 a month. Live-in caregivers paid roughly $325 a month for their accommodation and board in their employer's home, and this amount was deducted from their paycheque.

The experience of caregivers with their accommodations can be mixed. Sometimes, the employer is wealthy and has a beautiful, large house and a suite with a bathroom for their caregiver. Other caregivers do not have a room of their own. Several studies (Pratt 1999; Zaman 2006) have found that caregivers can be very uncomfortable in their employers' home, often living in spaces that violate the Live-in Caregiver Program (LCP) guidelines. Lilet had such an experience. She did not have her own room, but just used her employer's office room. Mary Jane said that she had shared accommodation. Rubia said she rented a place outside of her employer's home on weekends. Other caregivers were silent on this subject. Caregivers who did comment focused on the importance of privacy and were satisfied if they felt they had privacy in the employer's home. Tina, Santo, and Lenie all expressed satisfaction with their living arrangement because they felt they had privacy, while Yhor-am and Mary Jane were dissatisfied, feeling that they did not have enough privacy. The other main reason given for dissatisfaction with the living arrangement was that it was a noisy environment.

It is possible that some caregivers felt ambivalent about their housing because they could not claim their rooms and living arrangements as their own. Ruby noted why she was not satisfied with her accommodation: "It's not my own place." Other caregivers in the survey commented that, for them, being a caregiver was simply a stepping-stone to something better, a transitory period during which they accepted certain conditions, such as absence of skills security and employment security, lack of freedom, poor wages, long working hours, and possibly a lack of privacy or a decent room in their employer's home. To these participants, these unsatisfactory conditions in the workplace represented concessions made with a view to something better in the future, including permanent residency or, in the caregivers' term, "open visa."

Participants who were not live-in caregivers had more to say about their accommodation. Those who were satisfied with their accommodation frequently said that they lived in a good neighbourhood, had access to their community, and access to public transportation. It is clear that the Filipino community was a great source of psychological security for the participants. Since the participants were heavily reliant on public transportation, access was also very significant to them. Those who said that they were dissatisfied had comments relating to noise, neighbourhood safety, and malfunctioning utilities:

> Dante: [My place] is unsafe. [We] had a recent break-in in the home.
> Angel: [There has been an] increase in break-in incidents.
> Esmeralda: People living up [stairs] are very inconsiderate [and are] smoking marijuana.
> Oasis: [The] heat is not sufficient during winter. Some of the faucet[s] are leaking.
> Emmie: The house is very cold — the insulation is no good; the electrical is no good; the plumbing is no good. The landlord is not visiting the place.

Finding any kind of housing, let alone decent housing, can be difficult for Asian immigrants. They are often forced to live in substandard housing, which can have an impact on their health and thus make them even more vulnerable in terms of labour market security. Nelia spoke about the difficulty her family had in securing housing as recent immigrants:

> Nelia: We were walking through downtown. We were staying in the hotel.… In that three days, I spent more or less four hundred dollars. While staying in the hotel we went around the city and we saw this Filipino guy, Fred.… He said he knows of a two-bedroom house. We talked to the owner of the house, who came to our hotel, and we agreed to move to [that] house. This one here is our second rented house.
> Ed (Nelia's husband): We endured that place for eleven months.

Nelia and Ed were desperate to secure a place. They relied on word-of-mouth to find housing and did not attempt to find housing through more institutionalized channels. After a few months, they looked into BC Housing subsidies but did not pursue it for long:

> Ed: Well, we tried it out, but at this time, the BC Housing Authority had no vacancy for us. They said that they were giving priority to others.…

> But I don't like the BC housing program. It is like a permanent thing for the rest of your life. My plan is to have our own house eventually. Cecilia: Not really. You can always leave…. The only thing is, when you are renting privately, the landlord can arbitrarily raise the rent while BC Housing has a ceiling.
> Ed: Oh, I see. But you have to have an RRSP?
> Cecilia: No. That is not true.

Ed and Nelia's experience is probably quite common. Despite the fact that the majority of participants were of low income and could likely have qualified for subsidized housing, only two of the participants received housing subsidies. The reasons could include bureaucratic hurdles and, as Ed's comments show, lack of vacancies or accurate information, as well as a lack of interest on the part of the participants in pursuing what they considered to be temporary accommodation.

Use of Transportation

As Table 5 shows, participants relied heavily on public transportation. Fifty-two reported using the bus to get to work. Taking the bus usually cost between sixty and ninety-five dollars per month for a pass, or two dollars twenty-five cents each way at least — in either case, a substantial expense. Trips to the workplace and back can cost a minimum-wage earner an hour's wage. This survey was conducted before the 2010 Winter Olympics, which even before it started greatly increased the number of Skytrain riders. Overcrowding on the Skytrain may have been why several participants expressed dissatisfaction with this kind of transportation.

Table 5. Transportation Used by Participants to Get to Work*

Types of Transportation Used	Number
Bus	52
Sky train	22
Own transport	22
Walk to work	8
Get ride	5
Ride sharing	5

*Some participants used more than one mode of transport

Melanie talked about the unreliability of public transportation and the extra costs associated with relying on it:

> I take the bus. Sometimes, if I work in the early morning and there is no bus, I end up taking a taxi to my work. At the … store, if I end up working late, I would ask my mom to pick me up. But I have to help her buy the gas for the car. So I would end up spending close to one hundred dollars a month for my transportation and travel.

Some participants had very little access to public transportation and did not own their own means of transport, factors that compromised these participants' access to shopping, basic necessities, and the community. Barlyn, a caregiver who lived in Kelowna, said: "I walked for forty-three minutes going to the first bus stop."

Considering that it is very unlikely for live-in caregivers to have their own car, a lack of public transportation leaves caregivers as a group especially susceptible to isolation and compromises their access to the Filipino community and to help, should they need it. The large representation of caregivers in the survey may also explain the low numbers of participants reporting on the use of transport of any kind. As mentioned, most caregivers live where they work.

Child Care

Only twenty-two participants had non-adult children, a fairly low number that may be attributable to the large representation of caregivers, who are often young and single, in the survey. However, many caregivers leave their own family in the Philippines to work abroad. This was common among participants with children — eight had children still in the Philippines and supported them through remittance. Thus just fourteen families had children who required child care in Canada. Private child care was significantly relied upon by these participants. Interestingly, informal care — relying on family members and friends — was not usually utilized. This may be due to two facts: 1) very few participants had adult family members who could do child care, and 2) because they had recently arrived, few participants had had time to acquire friends who could help with child care. Participants did not appear to be satisfied with child-care arrangements. Many expressed enthusiasm for the demand for universal daycare and increased subsidized daycare, and this included participants who used private daycare or stayed at home to care for their children.

Table 6: Forms of Child Care (in percentages)

Forms of Child Care	Number
Child is in the Philippines	36
Stay-at-home parent	27
Private child care	23
Family/informal care	9
No child care (teenage children)	5
Total	100

There was no evidence of participants' children under the age of fifteen working. However, some participants had teenage or young adult children who worked. Some worked as caregivers, some in construction, and some in customer service, often making the minimum wage. These older children spent their income in various ways, including providing additional financial support for the family, both in BC and in the Philippines. In Canada, children of higher-income families often work for leisure income. However, participants of the survey mostly reported that their children worked in support of the family's basic needs, including the need to send remittance back to the Philippines. Here are samples of answers to the question, "What do your children do with their income?":

> Ron: Help with the rent.
> Ann: Send money to [the] Philippines, pay [for] school books, pay [for their] grad fees.

Gracy: Remittances and clothing.
Oasis: Help the family in financial problems.
Nelle: [They] help [with] financial needs. Sometimes [they] send money to the Philippines.

Remittance

Remittance is an invisible burden to racialized immigrants that non-racialized Canadians do not often consider. However, remittance has a significant impact on the economic security of Asian immigrants, as it places enormous strain on their financial resources. Remittances are used to support the housing, food, educational needs, and other necessities of family back in the country of origin. The survey participants immigrated largely for economic reasons, as discussed earlier, and this is further evidenced by their high rates of remittance. The Migration Policy Institute supports the theory that migration for economic reasons leads to high rates of remittance and mentions that when the migrant leaves for economic rather than political or social reasons, remittances are generally higher (Black 2003).

According to O'Neil (2003), globally, migrant workers sent home over US$6 billion in 2001. The Philippines ranked fourth among the countries with the highest total remittance in 2001 (Migration Policy Institute 2005). Thus, it is not surprising to find that the majority of survey participants (eighty) reported remitting funds to the Philippines. Fifty-six of the participants who sent remittances said that they did it on a monthly basis. A staggering eighty-four participants mentioned how difficult it was for them to try to save and send money. This statistic provides evidence of the increasing financial strain racialized families face and the economic insecurity they experience.

Access to Education in Canada

Due to economic insecurity, many Asian immigrants do not have access to and time for upgrading or further education to achieve skill security. Dante, a survey participant, alluded to this: "It takes too much to focus on education. Every minute, while working, always thinking where the money is going while I was getting paid so low. I couldn't stand it." Consequently, while seventeen participants reported receiving some post-secondary education in Canada, only ten of them had completed this level. Some participants found education too expensive. Linda commented: "[I] need better wages. [I] stopped training for home care because of decreasing funds. The program is six months and [costs] $10,000."

It was clear that participants found the upgrading process confusing, time-consuming, costly, and frustrating. The English language requirement of certain professions, like nursing, was a barrier often mentioned. Marelle noted her own experience: "I thought I could practise my nursing profession at once, but it's not the case due to a lot of barriers [including an English exam]." Most participants rated their English skills as good or very good, and one-third had received some form of language training.

There are barriers not only to obtaining education in Canada, but also to finding paid work that utilizes the training. For example, looking for a job for which a person is qualified can take a great deal of time. Most participants commented that they needed a job right away. This need often pushed them into a job for which they were overqualified and eventually started to erode the skills acquired through training or education. Jenny's experience is one example:

> Cecilia: But you are not using your training right now?
> Jenny: Because I don't have time right now. I have a certificate in cosmetology ... After I finished my training, I went back working full-time in that Japanese restaurant.

Survey Findings: Experiences of Various Levels of Insecurity in the BC Labour Market

For a majority of survey participants, whatever their educational qualifications and job experience, the first job in Canada was that of caregiver, and it was very difficult to move on from that job category later. Caregivers experienced extensive skills insecurity due to lack of recognition of their credentials and the inherently exploitative Live-in Caregiver Program (LCP). The following are excerpts from several caregivers' responses:

> Gig: I am not fully utilizing my skills and knowledge. It's very limiting — no outside jobs, no further studies, not much choice. It's a monotonous job.
> Bebot: It's a kind of work that is stagnant and [has] no challenges. It's like a prison cell that I [am] locked up inside, and I do nothing. There are no opportunities at all. It's a job that brings my self-esteem down, and [I get a] low income.
> Memy: I don't want to get old being a caregiver. I want a place of my own and [to] have a better living condition. I want to practise my nursing career in a medical setting or higher kind of job.
> Baby: My present job degrades my actual profession.
> Marelle: Working as a factory worker, dishwasher, and housekeeping attendant [is degrading], where in fact I am an experienced registered nurse in my country of origin and in [the] Middle East.

As these accounts illustrate, many caregivers felt a sense of dismay and sadness over the exploitation that occurs in the LCP. At the same time, other caregivers reported that they were satisfied with their jobs, perhaps because they are willing to accept their circumstances as a temporary situation, despite skills insecurity. This ambivalence is consistent with the general outlook of Asian immigrants who migrate to Canada with hopes, aspirations, and expectations for a better future.

A number of factors affecting participants' employment security in the BC labour market will be examined in the remainder of this section: their first jobs in Canada; their current jobs in Canada; the contradiction between unemployment and getting jobs quickly; work hours; wages; safety training; extended benefits; employment standards violations; knowledge of workers' rights and the ESA; and gender.

First Jobs in Canada

Only seven participants out of one hundred found jobs as professionals when they first came to Canada. Caregiving in the form of domestic work was the most common first job for the survey participants. The remaining participants worked first in one of the following categories: fast food, sales, and entry-level customer service, warehouse/production, or cleaning/janitorial jobs. These jobs tend to have low wages and inhospitable working conditions, and

Table 7: First Jobs in Canada

Type of Job	Number
Caregiving	69
Fast food/restaurant/entry level	12
Professional, others	7
Warehouse/production	5
Sales/customer service/entry level	4
Cleaning/janitorial	3
Total	100

the fact that participants held them despite their credentials is strong evidence of skills insecurity.

Current Jobs in Canada

Table 7 reported on participants' first jobs, so unemployment does not appear in the table. However, Table 8 shows participants' job status at the time of the survey ("current jobs"), and in it we see that unemployment is startlingly high, with sixteen participants unemployed and not in school. Table 8 also indicates that the majority of Filipino immigrants in the survey who were employed were still concentrated in the lower echelons of the workforce and thus had become trapped in a racialized space with its consequent economic insecurity.

Former caregivers generally moved into one of five categories: 1) maternity leave/stay-at-home parent;

Table 8: Current Jobs in Canada

Type of Job	Number
Domestic work	42
Unemployed	16
Care aide, dietary aide, etc.	8
Mobile	7
Fast food/restaurant/entry level	5
Cleaning/janitorial	4
Customer service/entry level	4
Warehouse/production	4
Unemployed student	3
Maternity leave/stay-at-home parent	3
Other	4
Total	100

2) unemployed/student; 3) mobile; 4) care aide or other type of aide worker; or 5) unemployed.

The "mobile" category includes participants who moved either into better jobs or into positions that offered future opportunities for promotions, wage increases, etc. For example, the mobile category includes Melanie, who from a crew member at a fast-food restaurant became a "swing" manager; Rachel, who worked at a fast-food restaurant for her first job and is now a private college instructor; Rivy, who was a banquet server and is now a web designer; Gemmie, who immigrated as a caregiver and is now a nurse; and Julia, a one-time caregiver and now a hairstylist. However, the number in the mobile category may not be as striking as it seems. For example, Mame, who now works as a nurse, has been in Canada since 1967, and there is evidence that at that time racialized immigrants had better success in finding work within their professions.

Care aides and dietary aides made up a significant portion of the sample's current jobs. There were no first jobs that were care aides, and the significant decrease in caregiving work is matched by a significant increase in aide work. Despite this movement, care aides and dietary aides were not put into the mobile category because it is questionable whether the move to aide work represents significant upward mobility. While care aids often earn more per hour than live-in caregivers, the work is often part-time or on-call. Of the eight care aides in the sample, four had only part-time or casual hours — an indication of employment insecurity.

The limited or illusory mobility experienced by Filipino immigrants does not enhance their basic security; rather the systemic process transforms them — along with other immigrants in the survey who are trapped in low-paid work — into an over-skilled proletariat.[2] Citizenship and Immigration Canada's program of bringing skilled immigrants to Canada is a failure because the federal government has not established processes to recognize these immigrants' training and experience in their country of origin.

The Contradiction of Unemployment and Getting Jobs Quickly

The unemployment level among the survey participants was very high, around twenty, or sixteen discounting those on maternity leave, those taking care of their own children, and those in school. However, the survey and also the interviews with participants found that many could obtain work rather quickly upon arrival — in the low-wage service and non-standard work sectors, and in non-communication jobs, i.e., jobs which do not require communication with clients or customers.[3] An interesting contradiction emerges. The Canadian Labour Congress has justified the need for minimum employment standards in the capitalist economy, as most workers are highly dependent upon their employment to support their families and the demand for jobs normally exceeds employer demands for labour (Canadian Labour Congress 2005). If this is the case, then why can racialized immigrants obtain these kinds of jobs so quickly? There must have been demand for their labour beyond the supply in the period of economic boom when the survey and interviews were conducted. However, if there were a labour shortage in this kind of work, the standards and wages would be expected to increase — which obviously did not happen — and unemployment would be expected to be low. There must be structural and systemic barriers that prevent these kinds of racialized jobs from paying what their market value should be in terms of wages and benefits and that keep unemployment in general high despite the economic boom.

The work in low-wage service sectors and non-standard sectors, including involuntary part-time and precarious, insecure, and deregulated jobs, is considered disguised unemployment (Canadian Labour Congress 2005). If work in low-wage service sectors and non-standard work are conceptualized as a kind of unemployment, the apparent contradiction between unemployment and quick access to jobs becomes more tangible. It is likely that people in these kinds of jobs experience the same kind of desperation that the unemployed do. The survey demonstrates that employers can continue to pay low wages, provide no benefits, and maintain terrible working conditions, and with the help of the 2002 ESA the amount of non-standard work continues to grow — and Asian and recent immigrant workers are caught in the trap.

Eighteen of the participants who have had more than one job in Canada have been at their current job for less than a year. Seventy-two of the participants were recent immigrants, having immigrated within the past five years. Recent immigrants appear likely to experience more job insecurity. One reason is that Asian immigrants are more likely than others in Canada to have non-standard work. For example, sixty participants either currently have or have had a contract agreement with their employer. Such work has an end-date, at which time the participant must find other work. Thus, the relationship between job insecurity, non-standard work, and recent immigrants promotes racialized and marginalized space in the workplace.

Work Hours at Current Jobs

Most survey participants reported working full-time — in fact, often more hours than would normally be considered full-time. Part-time or on-call work was not very common, with only twelve participants having these kinds of hours. This kind of work is often a way for employers to avoid giving full and extended benefits. Another twelve participants worked a kind of "part-time." These workers reported working more than thirty but not quite forty hours a week. Since their hours per week were below forty, these workers could be omitted from benefits too. This type of work includes fast food/restaurant and customer service, sectors known for having high rates of part-time employment. Further, in addition to some recipients reporting not having enough hours, other participants reported hours-abuse, such as forced overtime without overtime pay or without pay altogether.

Many participants reported having to do too much work for one person, and many said that they often suffered from exhaustion. Here are some excerpts from participant narratives:

Gretchen: If they ask me something, I can't say no!
Shamia: [My] workload is heavy — too many clients for short hours spent.
Melanie: Work [is] overloaded on only one person.
Dante: Not enough workers. [I am] overworked. I was working or doing [a] seven-people job.
Jessica: Staff shortage: workers have to do multi-tasking.
Emey: I do everything: child care — 3 kids — cooking, housekeeping. [My employers have] a huge house with [an] indoor pool.

The stress from overwork, injuries, and lack of personal time can have an impact on a person's ability to grow and enjoy life because it compromises life energy. There is no question that the nature of the work that recent Filipino immigrants do must have many debilitating effects on them.

Wages

For nearly every participant, the first job wage rate hovered around the minimum wage for that year (a little more or a little less). Not surprisingly, every participant who worked in fast food made minimum wages or just above, but never more than one dollar above. Those in cleaning/janitorial jobs and customer service made a similar amount. Some caregivers also received the minimum wage. One caregiver, Kresnke, noted that she received "officially eight dollars per hour, but in [reality] I am receiving below [the] minimum wage."

Sixteen participants reported receiving more than the training wage but less than eight dollars per hour in 2002, 2003, and 2004, when employers in BC could pay the training wage. As already noted above, participants could get jobs fairly quickly in those sectors where one would expect the training wage to be common, including fast food and customer service, because there was a labour shortage in those sectors. However, the fact that few participants overall received the training wage indicates that it is not a competitive wage during a time of economic boom. Of the sixteen participants who said they received wages lower than eight dollars an hour, two worked in fast food, two in customer service, one in cleaning/janitorial, and one as a receptionist. Of these sixteen participants, there was evidence of abuse of the training wage in all but one case. Furthermore, six of these sixteen participants worked as caregivers. This clearly defies the legislation since the training wage did not apply to caregivers. Part of the reason the training wage was susceptible to being used in an abusive way was that the BC government kept no statistics or information on how many workers received the training wage, nor on whom the workers were. Furthermore, as will be discussed in Chapter Four, many people were unaware of the changes made to the ESA and how the training wage was supposed to operate. Workers who do not know their rights are more easily abused.

Thirty-seven of those who reported receiving a training wage also said that they had not received any training, although this was the ostensible impetus for the government's introduction of a training wage. Furthermore, half of these participants reported not receiving a wage increase after five hundred hours. Three were fired or laid off while receiving the training wage. Another startling finding is that 25 percent of those who received the training wage were unemployed at the time of the survey. It is not clear what the correlation may be, though it does signal that there were some systemic problems with the training wage.

Safety Training

While thirty-nine participants received on-the-job safety training, many did not. Sixty-one either did not receive on-the-job safety training (thirty-six participants) or did not respond to this question in the survey (twenty-five participants). This indicates that at least one quarter and possibly almost two-thirds of the participants had no on-the-job safety training, which raises concerns for Asian immigrants' safety in the workplace.

Extended Benefits

Approximately one-third of the participants received some form of extended benefits for their first job, as can be seen in Table 9. Since basic medical benefits were mandatory, extended benefits included dental, overtime pay, paid training, paid leave, sick leave, maternity leave, pension plan, and RRSP. While almost half the participants received overtime pay on their first job, approximately a third received dental coverage or paid leave, and about a quarter received sick leave or access to a pension plan. Few received paid training, maternity leave, or contributions to a registered retirement savings plan (RRSP) program. Participants who did not receive extended benefits were clearly unhappy. For example, Yhor Am, Raven, and Gretchen all specifically mentioned they were dissatisfied with their jobs for this reason.

Table 9: Extended Benefits Received for First Jobs

Type of benefits	% of respondents received
Overtime	46
Paid leave	36
Dental	32
Sick leave	25
Pension plan	25
Paid training	17
Maternity leave	16
RRSP	10

Benefits are an important part of basic economic security. Not only ability to work, but also level of happiness and life satisfaction are affected when a worker lacks extended benefits and cannot afford prescription drugs or dental work. Lack of a pension plan and opportunity to make RRSP contributions means that workers are likely to experience economic insecurity well into their old age. Obtaining benefits was clearly of utmost importance to the participants, who expressed the most satisfaction with their jobs if they received extended benefits.

Employment Standards Violations

Many participants recounted violations of workers' rights. Several caregivers described abuse violating not only Live-in Caregiver Program guidelines, which stipulate that the caregiver is entitled to her own room, free time, and amenities, but also the employment contract and the *Employment Standards Act*.

> Rosa: [My] employer didn't treat me well. I worked twenty-two hours a day. [I] slept with [my elderly patient] in the same bedroom, [and] they didn't give me a spare key to the apartment. I was not able to take my shower inside the apartment. I shower[ed] at [the] parking lot recreation room's shower room. I was really belittled by my employer.
> Dorothy: [I have] twelve hours' work time but [only] ten and a half hours are paid.
> Sunshine: [I was] so overworked. I didn't complain because I was new here [in Canada].

Many participants were reluctant to report violations. Caregivers especially may be reluctant as their permanent residency status depends on their completing twenty-four months of live-in care work, and they are thus dependent on the good will of their employers. Another reason is that racism makes Asian immigrants vulnerable and compromises their economic security in terms of the wages they can command, their safety at work, and their sense of self through voice and representation. Except for "lack of training," racism was the barrier most cited by participants, although there was no question on racism in either the survey or the interviews.

Despite the many kinds of workers' rights violations experienced, participants were less likely to report such violations than to report when wages were unpaid. This suggests systemic discouragement, with participants focusing on those violations that affected them the most. Here are samples of excerpts from participant responses:

> Jen: They didn't pay us in the right day and time.
> Rambo: [They] didn't pay enough money on the paycheque.
> Ann: They would not pay enough hours on the paycheque.
> Pete: [T]here was a shortage on my paycheque.
> Nitz: Very long hours without pay. Work on my days off.

These and other participants' statements provided further evidence that immigrant workers are likely to focus on their most immediate needs — income security — rather than on other rights such as employment security, voice, and the representational security to which they are entitled. As discussed earlier, low-income workers are often at the maximum of threats to their security that they can deal with. While other security can be compromised, a steady income is of utmost necessity for these workers.

Knowledge of Workers' Rights and the ESA

Although thirty-four of the participants reported that their workers' rights had been violated, only nineteen reported having complained about the violation. However, since only sixty-nine said that they were aware of workers' rights in their workplaces, the number of participants who experienced violations could be higher. Most participants did not have adequate knowledge of workers' rights because there was little access to information about these rights in the workplace. Twenty-three participants had seen workers' rights posted in the workplace, and forty-one, or just under half, reported having seen the ESA posted or having heard of the Act. It is not surprising that very few (ten) had heard of changes to the ESA.

Participants who had heard of the *Employment Standards Act* were asked what it is. Their responses were usually either that the ESA guaranteed workers' rights in general, or the ESA focused on wages and hours but not on other rights or security. Here are some sample answers to this question about the ESA:

> Chamz: It states the rights of an employee.
> Shamia: It's about your rights as an employee.
> Raven: The employee-employer contract should be within the provincial *Employment Standards Act*.
> Rosa: This is the agency that will help us under the LCP program about our rights and compensation that we should get from our employer.
> Ashley: [A] caregiver will work eight hours a week, forty hours weekly, [and] will have overtime pay.
> Pearly: Eight hours [a day.] More than eight hours equals overtime.
> Maryjane: I only know like how much the wage [should be] per hour.
> Aurean: Work paid is minimum wage.

A few participants confused collective agreements with the ESA. Some participants noted that they had heard of the ESA but were not sure what it contained.

> Mary Jane: Honestly, I don't know much about this.
> Rachel: [I have] heard of the Act but don't know what it states.

While it is difficult for a survey to capture how extensive participants' knowledge is of legislation like the ESA, it is likely that many participants were not fully aware of their rights and were thus susceptible to abuse. With the changes in 2002 to the ESA, the susceptibility can only be worsened, as employers are no longer required to take any initiative in informing workers of their rights by posting rights information in the workplace.

Gender

Partly because caregivers were heavily represented in the survey sample, 89 percent of participants were women.

The survey found that male and female participants who had immigrated recently had very similar labour market experiences in terms of wages, work hours, workers' rights violations, and unemployment. In fact, the proportion of women unemployed at the time of the survey was almost equal to the proportion of men unemployed in the total survey, even though the two often took on different kinds of work. For example, men were more likely to work in warehouse/production and janitorial work. Interestingly, the proportion of men in the mobile category was also almost equal to the proportion of women in the mobile category in the total survey. This suggests that race more than gender is a factor in recent Asian immigrants' experiences in the labour market.

In some married couples, one took on a "breadwinner" role, and the other stayed at home and looked after the children. Seven of the twenty female participants who were unemployed said that their spouses were supporting them. In contrast, none of the male participants reported being supported by a spouse.

Summary

This survey has provided a comprehensive demographic view of Asian immigrants, and more specifically of Filipino immigrants. The survey of one hundred participants and short citations from in-depth and focus group interviews demonstrate that the neo-liberal restructuring of the ESA has not only deteriorated work conditions but has contributed to marginalizing Asian immigrants in the workplace and has unwittingly promoted racialized workspaces that eliminate basic security for Asian immigrants. Further, the survey has demonstrated that many Asian immigrants live in the Downtown Eastside area of Vancouver, a space that is already demarcated for the marginalized population in the city who live in desperate poverty. The International Labour Organization's comprehensive program of basic security is an illusion for Asian immigrants in Canada when one considers their housing, transportation, current jobs, remittances, and substandard workplace conditions. Further, restructuring of the ESA in BC has had far-reaching, adverse consequences for economic security and workplace environments for Asian immigrants, who already face barriers in the labour market.

Notes

1. De-skilling among immigrants is well recognized and documented by many studies (Bakan and Staiulis 1994; Pratt 1999; Zaman 2006) and hence was not explored in this survey.
2. A previous study (Zaman 2006) showed that a few racialized immigrants who had been in Canada long-term fared fairly well in terms of job security, not only in terms of obtaining their first job in the profession for which they were trained, but also in obtaining skills security with the post-secondary education they had acquired in the Philippines. This survey did not have similar findings — those Filipino immigrants who arrived before 1980 obtained first jobs similar to those of recent immigrants, such as

fast food, dishwashing, and caregiving positions. However, the current survey sampled working-age immigrants, and many of those who arrived before 1980 immigrated as children or youth and thus did not obtain any secondary education in their country of origin. Their first jobs in Canada may reflect their youth to a greater extent and barriers to employment security to a lesser extent. It seems that, in general, recent immigrants and youth obtain similar kinds of work in the low-wage service industry. This supports my earlier finding that "immigrant women with a university degree have an employment rate almost equivalent to a Canadian-born high school dropout" (Zaman 2006: 53).

3.   A worker who prepares beef patties in the kitchen in a fast food industry is an example of a non-communication job. A participant in my research has coined this term in her first language, Bangla.

Chapter 4

Reproduction of Racialized Space

Narratives about Dimensions of Security

The survey of one hundred Filipino immigrants analyzed in Chapter Three facilitated the discovery of racialized immigrants' average wage rates and hours, housing, transportation, benefits, child care, and other features. In order to add a more nuanced analysis of the economic security of Asian immigrants in BC, twenty-four Filipino-ancestry participants and twelve Pakistani-ancestry immigrants were interviewed from 2005 to 2008, i.e., three to six years after the restructuring of the *Employment Standards Act* (ESA) in 2002. See the first chapter for details on the interviewers and the methodology. My previous research (Zaman 2006) with Bangladeshi-ancestry and Indian-ancestry immigrants has further sharpened the analysis for this chapter. These individual and focus group perspectives added depth to the definition of racialized and gendered spaces generated from the interviews in my previous research and revealed new information of their own.

In this chapter, the results of the intensive interviews and the major findings of the survey are illustrated to demonstrate the considerable economic insecurity many Asian immigrants in BC encounter. This economic insecurity is produced by multiple factors including the type of first jobs obtained after arriving in Canada, the demand that recent immigrants have Canadian job experience, the lack of voice and representation in the workplace, and the absence of the posting of the ESA due to its 2002 restructuring. The findings described in this chapter show that the changes to the ESA have exacerbated economic insecurity and consequently helped produce and reproduce racialized space for many Asian immigrants in BC.

A Brief Profile: In-Depth Interviews

To conceal identities, the names of the participants are fictitious; however, they chose their own pseudonyms and identified their gender. In all, there were twenty-five women and eleven men. One of the participants was a transwoman who undertook her transition after migrating to Canada. From the interviews, some gendered variations in work experiences were evident. Men's first jobs in Canada were mostly in production or in warehouses, whereas women began working in stores and restaurants and as caregivers for the elderly, children, and people with mental and physical challenges. Men's workplaces were more hazardous than women's in terms of the use of chemicals and machinery, while women's workplaces were more likely to pose hazards of sexual discrimination and other forms of abuse. For example, one caregiver had to endure terrifying sexual advances from her employer, and another, the transwoman, was fired after the employer found out about her transition. A higher proportion of men than women reported labour mobility in terms of wages and occupations. One explanation may be that women had more child-rearing responsibilities and were more susceptible to gender-based systemic and structural discrimination. At the same time, some women, not their husband[1]/spouse, were the "breadwinners" for their households. This "exchange" of roles seemed to correspond mostly to the period soon after arrival rather than later in the settlement process.

As with the survey participants, the in-depth interview participants were recent arrivals to Canada, having arrived within the past fifteen years, and many were very recent, having arrived within the past five years. As immigrants to Canada, the participants fell into three categories: independent, skilled, or family members.[2] Most of these participants immigrated as a family member under the independent/skilled category. In other words, the participants came under Citizenship and Immigration Canada's comprehensive economic category, indicating that Asian immigrants are expected to contribute to the Canadian economy. This is unlike the survey participants where the majority migrated under the Live-in Caregiver Program.

The in-depth interview participants were almost exclusively very well educated, most having a bachelor's degree in a field for which there is currently a demand in Canada, such as engineering and nursing. This finding reflects the current emphasis on the skilled category in Canada, where such labour is much needed. However, the erosion of immigrants' skills and the lack of recognition for their credentials, which are well documented in the literature (Grant and Sweetman 2004; Li 2003; Picot 2004; Zaman 2004), mean that the interview participants were largely unable to find employment in the field for which they had trained.

The remainder of this chapter examines these participants' experiences after they arrived in Canada. Through interview testimonies, the seven sections present examples of what the participants experienced in terms of the following: 1) basic security; 2) labour market security; 3) income security; 4) employment security; 5) job security; 6) skills security; and 7) voice and representation security.

Basic Security: An Illusion Shattered

Basic security is a guiding principle for a liberal-democratic welfare state like Canada. Many recent immigrants assume that they will find basic security in Canada but soon discover that basic security is an illusion that shatters as their savings deplete and the days pass by. The participants' narrations indicate unique and individualized experiences in the labour market, although with some commonalities. The following five brief narratives from Jenny, Bong, Glecy, Sid, and Jabeen demonstrate how economic insecurity is embedded in Asian immigrants' lives. These accounts range from a teenager who was supposed to attend a school to a professional who struggled with credential recognition. These participants' stories in their own voices appear throughout this chapter and in subsequent chapters.

Lack of Job Security: Immediate Financial Need

In 2000, shortly after finishing high school, Jenny came to Canada as a teenager sponsored by her mother. Immediately after her arrival, Jenny desperately searched for a job because she needed to contribute to her family financially. One day she walked into a restaurant asking about work, and they hired her immediately without giving her an interview. She had no idea what her hourly wage rate, working conditions, duties, or benefits would be. Jenny soon felt overworked because she was putting in more than eight-hour days, six days a week. When she asked about her wage, the employer told her she would be paid just four dollars an hour. Jenny quit after two weeks on the job. She then started helping her mother in a caregiving centre. The work was casual, and the payment was under the table — not reported by either side. This under-the-table working environment runs counter to the ideology of the welfare state.[3]

Jenny next found two part-time jobs — one at a supermarket and another at a restaurant — and was even able to send remittances to her family in the Philippines in addition to contributing to her family in Canada. Jenny also found the time to take training in cosmetology. However, after completing the training, she could not find work in the field. She went back to working in a restaurant, and she also delivered food and did other combinations of part-time jobs. At the time of the interview, she was employed at a chain food store. She had been on the job for only three months, and she had not yet been paid enough to meet her basic needs. Jenny was again looking for something better.

Occupational Mobility and Utilization of Service Providers

Bong — a man in his early thirties and an experienced electrical engineer in the Philippines — arrived in Canada in 2003 with his wife and three children. After his arrival, he attended seminars and sought advice from S.U.C.C.E.S.S.[4] as he found it impossible to get a job. He eventually obtained a loan from the provincial government to undertake a computer programming course. Although his wife had continuous part-time jobs, he also had to take up various part-time jobs to support the family. It took Bong two years to get a job in his new field, computer programming. Finally, he found a job in the technology sector through an internet search. In this job, he received benefits and the company even paid for educational upgrading pertinent to the job. Bong considered himself "lucky" for getting this job, but, as he pointed out, this job was not related to his original field, engineering.

Whose Responsibility? Caught Between the CIC and the ESB

Glecy arrived in Canada via the LCP in 2002. As a live-in caregiver, she was unaware of her rights. Her employer asked her to babysit the neighbour's children and never paid Glecy for this extra work, although the neighbour paid the employer. According to Glecy, her employer smoked marijuana in the home, entered her room at night, and made repeated sexual advances that frightened her. She tried desperately to find another employer so that she would be able to meet her twenty-four month work requirement.[5] Unable to find another job for a month, she had to stay working with the same family, and consequently the sexual advances continued. One day, her cousin visited and found Glecy working on the roof of the house, a task that a live-in caregiver is certainly not required to do. Shocked, the cousin quickly helped Glecy find another employer. She was never paid for the month that she worked for her first employer.

Glecy's next employer made her work more than eight hours a day. When her employer and she had a disagreement, Glecy decided to find another employer. This third employer did not live up to their contract in terms of wages, snooped in Glecy's private papers, threw out her mail, and submitted an incorrect T4 tax slip. The Employment Standards Branch (ESB) told Glecy that this was a Canada Immigration and Citizenship (CIC) issue. CIC told her that it was an ESB issue. Caught between bureaucratic disputes, Glecy ended up paying a $1,300 tax bill.

After Glecy's twenty-four month residency requirement ended, she applied for Employment Insurance (EI). She tried working at a fast-food chain restaurant, but they told her she would only be paid the training wage, six dollars hourly. During the interview, Glecy reported that she babysat and worked part-time in a store, lived in subsidized housing, and sent remittances to her family in the Philippines.

Chronic Insecurity Denies Basic Security

Sid, a thirty-five-year-old who had a Bachelor of Commerce in Accounting and had worked in a bank for thirteen years, migrated with her husband and three children as an independent immigrant in 2005. She and her husband were told to bring $20,000 for the family — i.e., $4,000 per person — to Canada. After their arrival, they stayed with one family for a few days and then shared a basement suite with another family.

Noticing a "Now Hiring" sign while shopping, Sid approached the store owner and immediately got the job. She started working without a workplace orientation and without a social insurance number. Her travel time to work was over one hour, and she had to juggle her schedules with her husband's so that the children were cared for. When, after some time, she did not have her social insurance number due to processing delays, her employer fired her. Her husband told her that she needed to take care of their children anyway.

At the time of the interview, Sid's husband's job as a janitor supported the family, with a total monthly income of $980. He had not been working there long enough to collect any benefits. They still shared the basement suite with another family, with the five members of Sid's family living in two bedrooms. During her interview, Sid said that at Christmas she had gone to the Christmas Bureau because the family's low income qualified them for a twenty-five-dollar grocery store gift certificate per family member. Unfortunately, she was not told that she had to take proof that she had a husband, so received just four certificates instead of the much-needed five.

Conflicts, Dilemmas, and Erosion of Skills and Basic Security

Jabeen came to Canada in 2002 as a principal applicant accompanied by her husband, a senior civil servant in their country of origin, and four children. Jabeen had a PhD in psychology from an Australian university and ten years of teaching experience in her country of origin. In Canada, at the time of the interview she had been working as a part-time family counsellor for five years, and her husband worked, at least at first, as a security officer. The following account demonstrates how Jabeen's basic security was compromised by conflicts, dilemmas, and erosion of skills:

> My husband worked here for about eight months, and then he left and went back to [country of origin].... We fought a lot during [the time my husband was in Canada]. He was very tense, and I was also. We thought we had made a wrong decision [by coming to Canada]. We also used to blame each other for what had happened. We had both had excellent jobs and a marvellous life style [in our country of origin], which we regretted leaving. He went back a couple of times. During that time I had to take care of everything: the kids, home, and job. We had a lot of quarrels [and I used to say to my husband] why don't you sacrifice as well for [the] kids? Why have you left all of us here and gone back to save your job?... He was of a point of view that we should all come back and settle in [country of origin], to which our kids did not agree. Due to all these tensions, I could not explore anything for myself and was stuck at this job where I am right now. I feared that if I lose this [job] how will I manage my kids and home?

Jabeen's story indicates how absence of basic security creates dilemmas, conflicts, and tensions within a family. Her husband's decision to return to their country of origin placed her in the position of being the sole earner for the family. As a result, she was stuck in a part-time job without any chance of exploring upgrading in her field or finding a full-time position as she was also the child-care provider at home.

Basic Security Compromised

The above five brief narrations by Asian immigrants demonstrate that basic security after migration can be compromised in multi-dimensional ways, and each immigrant's story is unique. Of these five participants, Bong, with the help of immigration settlement services, achieved a sort of occupational mobility although he lacked job satisfaction. However, Jenny, Sid and Jabeen struggled to meet basic needs. Jenny, as a young immigrant, skipped school and took training to upgrade her skills while holding several part-time jobs both to support her family in Canada and to send remittances to family in the Philippines. As a mother of three children, Sid had to obtain food vouchers from an agency in order to provide for her family over the holidays. Even with a PhD in psychology, Jabeen was forced to sacrifice her professional training and do a part-time job to achieve basic security. In addition, the frustrations associated with trying to achieve basic security created conflicts and tensions between her and her husband. Glecy, who came to Canada as a migrant domestic worker,[6] had to deal with unscrupulous employers during the two years of residency required, then was caught in a bureaucratic tangle that resulted in her having to pay a hefty income tax bill.

These five immigrants' testimonies support the International Labour Organization's assertion (2004: 5) that basic security is worsening for the already vulnerable — ordinary workers, women, and other disadvantaged groups including racialized immigrants:

> Our position starts from the assertion that every person everywhere has a right to basic security. ... It means limiting the uncertainties people face in their daily lives ... providing a social environment in which people ... feel they belong to a range of communities, and have a fair and good opportunity to live a decent life and to ... decent work.

Without basic security, Asian immigrants in Canada do not feel settled and do not feel integrated into Canadian society. Some, like Jabeen's husband, return to their original country, with all the negative consequences that can involve, including the break-up of families. It must be noted that although immigration literature has a major focus on settlement and integration,[7] research and publications on commuting relationships and emigration from Canada are not readily available.

Labour Market Security:
Intersections of Underemployment and Unemployment

The International Labour Organization (ILO) (2004: 124–27) summarized the global picture of labour market security by making a regional and demographic comparison and in doing so produced some interesting findings: that unemployment is gendered; that seniors and youth experience greater levels of unemployment; and that migration is implicated in unemployment. However, the ILO's findings did not adequately illustrate the relationship between unemployment, migration, and globalization.

In fact, little attention has been paid to the significant phenomenon of migration/immigration and labour market security. Further, conventional indicators are not reliable in measuring true labour market security. For example, the official low unemployment rates in Canada conceal both the pauperization of work and the actual unemployment rate among racialized immigrants. Indeed, the category "visible minority" masks the nature of Asian immigrants' experience of labour market participation. Also, it is too frequently presumed that it is desirable to have a very high "employment rate" and to maximize the number of "jobs" despite their being precarious. Labour market insecurity can arise for Asian immigrants because they are obliged to find jobs quickly in their new country. At the same time as they look for work, most are caring for children/family members, doing community/volunteer work, and perhaps re-training.

Participants' experiences revealed the dynamics of labour market security for Asian immigrants in Canada. The participants can be divided into two "streams" of experiences upon arrival with regard to obtaining jobs. Some experienced a long bout of unemployment while looking for a job relating to their education, training, and experience. Others obtained jobs quite quickly, sometimes as soon as a few days after arriving in Canada. The latter noted that they had to seek jobs right away out of financial necessity. However, almost all participants ended up with the same kind of low-paid jobs. The majority of participants were trained and well educated, and most of them migrated under the skilled category. Participants' experiences with finding jobs suggests that recent immigrants experience unemployment less frequently than they experience severe downward occupational mobility.

Asian immigrants who experienced the longest periods of unemployment sought jobs for which they had been trained and educated outside of Canada. Most of these immigrants sent out many applications. The majority experienced frustration at being unable to obtain jobs in their professions, which ranged from teaching to engineering to nursing. According to the participants, every employer they approached was looking for "Canadian experience." With little exception, these participants were discouraged from seeking jobs for which they had been trained. Once these participants gave up on looking for this type of work, they usually found jobs quickly, almost exclusively in the low-wage service and production sectors. Joseph's story provides an example:

> Yes, [engineering firms] and related companies. I must have sent out over eighty applications and résumés.… I did get some interviews. But it all ended at interviews. One time I was interviewed by a company that does electroplating for microchips. They toured me around the company and asked a few questions. But that was all. When I asked if they wanted me to start working for the company, they said that they were still doing some more interviews, and they would call me. That's all. They never called back.… This was continuous. I still do it now. Even if I am now working as a security officer, and I am studying, I still continue to look for a job [in the engineering field].

Although most participants needed to obtain work quickly upon arrival due to financial pressures, there was a real need for their labour in the labour market — as long as their labour fell into certain categories. This was evident by how quickly participants could obtain low-wage service and production types of jobs.

Jobs were often sourced through informal networks, such as through connections with family and friends, as opposed to formal networks like immigrant and settlement services. Some participants did utilize services from the Immigrant Services Society, such as résumé help or training for a specific skill, such as computer science. A few participants used the internet to find job postings and submit résumés. The following are examples of job searches by very recent immigrants:

> Regan: When we arrived here, my father started looking for friends. One of them was working in a factory making jackets. He referred me to that company, and that's how I started working…. I was worried about expenses as I had to work and contribute right away. My mom's income sometimes is not sufficient to cover our needs. That is why I was forced to work immediately.

> Bong: I was there [at S.U.C.C.E.S.S] for one month straight — for one month at eight hours a day. [Finally] I was able to get this job in the electronics field. It took me two years to be able to get this job that is related to my training…. I got it through the internet. I saw it and I e-mailed. I do this every time I have free time. I just keep sending my résumé. This company called me up and said if I was interested … they would hire me. They interviewed me by phone in the afternoon. I went there for a personal interview, and that's how I got the job…. [It's hard], especially if you have no network. Like the place where I am working now. There are also Filipinos there, and they ask how I got the job there. Of course, I tell them that I just applied. They said that I was fortunate to get the job. Most got their jobs through networking. They already knew people inside who recommended them for their job. Because you see, if there is someone in the company who recommends you, you have a good chance of getting hired. [The employers] give people who recommend someone a minimum of five hundred dollars…. If they have an opening and if you recommend someone and he/she gets accepted, you get a minimum five hundred dollars as a recommendation fee.

Although Bong's description of a five hundred dollar recommendation fee is surprising, his account has been endorsed by other participants. It is evident that networking, personal connections, and even the Asian immigrant community play major roles in locating jobs, especially first-time jobs.

Some participants found jobs in what may be called haphazard ways. In Ronnie's case, she walked into a store to buy groceries and walked out with a job:

> I did not do anything. I think I was just lucky. I went into this vegetable and fruit store to buy something, and one of the sales ladies asked me if I wanted a part-time job…. Of course I was interested in the job if there was one available. So, she asked me to return to the store for the job. I went back and they interviewed me. They liked me and accepted

me right away. I just gave them my résumé, after which they just asked me to sign the form.... My designation is store retailer or storekeeper.

Ronnie's experience is evidence of labour shortages in certain kinds of work in Canada, such as retail. Only a store desperate to hire someone would approach customers to see if they needed a job. Or perhaps the assumption is that every racialized immigrant is looking for a job in a store! The following account from Sid further shows that Asian immigrants often quickly land first jobs in retail:

> Well, we were driving around Richmond. The cousin of my husband was on leave for seven days. He drove us all over the Lower Mainland. My son liked toy cars. S [the cousin] remembered this and took us to a store. So, we went there. When we arrived there, we saw a sign "Now Hiring." The cashier was Filipina. S asked if they were hiring, and the cashier said yes, that they were hiring. She even asked him if he knew someone who would be interested. S said that he knew someone who had just arrived, but still had not received her social insurance number. The woman said that it was all right — the social insurance number could follow as long as she had applied for it. Of course, they brought me up and asked me to fill in the application form. They asked us to return the following day. I did not realize that it was very far from where we live. It was more than a one-hour trip. But it was okay. After I submitted my application form, William (the guy in the store) asked me to start immediately. Of course, I did not know anything. But I agreed to start immediately. So, I started the following day. I enjoyed it. Almost all of my co-employees there were Filipinos.... Yes. We were paid eight dollar per hour. But it is just part-time work for me — in the afternoon until the closing. This is the time when there are lots of customers.

The above narratives indicate that the immigrant community, in this case the Filipino community, is an important source of job information. Many participants reported that the majority of their co-workers were Filipino, a fact demonstrating that a racialized space has been created for Filipino immigrants. Most often, a racialized space is fragmented and segmented along the lines of country of origin, ethnicity, and language. Interestingly, religion (for example, Christianity, which is the Filipino immigrants' religion, or Islam, which is the Pakistani immigrants' religion) in the workplace was not mentioned in the interviews. Many participants noted that their employers sought out Filipino workers because they "don't complain," and "work harder than others," and are willing to accept a lower wage. This very concept of ethnicity as well as country of origin among racialized workers makes the notion of solidarity and collective bargaining in the workplace more difficult. Indeed, this notion of ethnicity for a specific job reproduces and sustains a racialized workplace that is overwhelmingly evident in the lower echelons of the labour market in Canada.

It is also apparent from the interviews that the kinds of jobs and the size of the company play significant roles in terms of the manner in which recent immigrants are hired. For example, a number of participants worked at a chain food store that seems to have an institutionalized and systematic application process. Other businesses, like small restaurants, often did not interview participants or ask for résumés. In these situations, many participants did not have a good sense of the jobs they were going to be performing, or even what their wage rate or hours would be. Jenny, whose situation was presented earlier in this chapter, was paid far below minimum wage and did not find out about it until two weeks after starting the job. Without an interview, there is little opportunity for a prospective employee to ask questions about the nature of the work and make an informed decision about whether to work there. As will be discussed in more detail later in this chapter, the changes made to the *Employment Standards Act* in 2002 have made it easier for employers to have more temporary, and consequently fewer full-time employees, and so has further compromised labour market security.

Income Security: Shifting Costs from Employers to Workers

Income security is perhaps the most important and immediate form of economic security. Income security includes many things other than wages, such as employer- or state-provided benefits (medical, dental, subsidized transportation, etc.) that have a monetary value. The ILO (2004) argues that a wide range of income sources is necessary for income security, so that if any one source fails, there are others to fall back on. However, the ILO notes that the social contract between workers and employers developed after World War II to provide protection has steadily diminished. Further, in BC, the government's restructuring of the ESA has whittled away income security, helping to shift costs from employers to workers.

There was some variation in the hourly rate paid to the interview participants depending on their jobs. For their first jobs in Canada, the majority of participants made the minimum wage or close to it — eight dollars per hour in BC at the time, one of the lowest minimum wages in Canada despite BC's booming economy. Workers in retail and hand-harvesting made the minimum wage, and workers in security jobs, care aide jobs, and production sometimes made more, upwards of fifteen dollars per hour. The few immigrants among the participants who were working in skilled jobs were making decent wages by the time they were interviewed, but they had started out working in the low-wage sectors upon arrival in Canada. Participants with children sometimes made as little as $1,000 a month. The prevalence of low wages suggests a widespread lack of income security among the participants.

Lila's narration is an example of income security becoming precarious: "It depends on the call. ... The number of hours is often not enough. But after January of this year, there was a slowdown. So I did not have any work. ... Now, we are back in full gear again after this summer. Now, I can start again buying some stuff for the house." Lila's narration reveals income insecurity — precarious work hours and the inability to "buy things for the house" in slower times. (The situation becomes even worse if someone is laid off before qualifying for Employment Insurance, as Loy's account illustrates in the next section.)

To maintain income security, several participants took more than one part-time job, each at close to the minimum wage. Edgardo's account demonstrates this point:

> I was [doing] cleaning work there. It was a graveyard shift. I gave my résumé to my aunt to give to my employer. It was a cleaning company. I was also working there for eight hours per shift…. It was the same as my previous employment. I was also working five days a week for eight hours a day. My wage was $8.75 per hour. It was also casual work. But if you wanted to be permanent, they would accept you because they were also looking for permanent workers. After I was there for one month, I applied at the hospital and got accepted. So, I ended up with two jobs.

Edgardo's narration reveals that in order to have an adequate level of income, he needed to hold more than one job. Both jobs were temporary and part-time, and thus did not have employer-provided benefits such as medical, dental, and subsidized transportation. The very nature of these jobs shifts costs such as medical and dental from the employer to the employee. In Edgardo's case, as for many other immigrants, the restructuring of the ESA provides far more flexibility to the employers by creating more non-standard jobs that do not provide many, if any, benefits.

According to the immigrants interviewed, benefits are extremely important. Some suggested that immigrants make a "trade-off," taking and staying in an unsatisfactory job if they are receiving benefits. These immigrants are also more likely to stay in a job with benefits despite problems and even if they could make a higher wage elsewhere. Benefits are directly related to job satisfaction; in other words, those who received benefits also seemed likely to express satisfaction with their work. Those who did not receive benefits talked about how expensive it was for them to pay their provincial MSP (Medical Services Plan) premium and go to the dentist. William, a participant in a focus group, eventually found work as a technologist. His responses during a focus group exemplify the correlation between job satisfaction and benefits:

> William: I work at BT.
> Ted: What position were you hired for?
> William: I started working there on January 3, 2005, as a technologist.
> Ted: How many hours do you work daily?
> William: I work seven and a half hours every day.
> Ted: Are your hours flexible?
> William: Yes. I work five days a week. I get the weekends. I am paid

above the minimum wage. I also get the benefits of the company —
medical, dental, vacation pay, etc.
Ted: Are you aware of workers' rights in your workplace?
William: Yes. They gave [us] some documents to read about the
conditions in the workplace. But I was not asked to sign anything.
Ted: In terms of work satisfaction, are you satisfied with your current
job?
William: Yes. At least I am able to practise the profession that I trained
for in [my country of origin]. The salary and benefits are adequate for
my needs and family. I find it a rewarding experience. I am gaining
experience here in Canada. My first job at [a window company] did
not satisfy me. I felt exploited in that job.

Despite their seeking out jobs with benefits, many participants did not know
the exact nature of those benefits. For example, some participants were not sure
if they received vacation pay. This lack of clarity may be related to participants'
preoccupation with wages and hours, i.e., income security. As Jenny noted, "In
my dishwashing job, I don't know if I am getting any vacation.… I don't mind
about this. My only concern is that I'll get my salary right. I don't know much
about my vacation pay." This attitude is indicative of a lack of economic security,
which is characterized by a persistent preoccupation with meeting the most
basic needs. Once basic needs like housing and food were met, then participants
could start familiarizing themselves with benefits or seeking jobs that provided
them with benefits. It appears that economic security, and its inverse, insecurity,
have exponential effects. In other words, insecurity seems to generate even more
insecurity while security seems to generate even more security.

Employment Security

The International Labour Organization (ILO) (2004) has defined employment
security — highlighting its subjective nature and outlining some trends — and
formulated some indexes to measure informalization and employment security.
The ILO (2004: 138–39) rightfully points out that weakened legislation and
structural changes affect employment security: "Traditionally, public sectors
provided workers with a greater and more formalized sense of employment
security than public firms. [Currently there is a] tendency for public sectors
to shrink." This is clearly the case with the BC provincial Liberal government's
policies. For example, the privatization of hospital work and cuts to the public
sector show that the BC government is participating in a global trend away from
employment security (Stinson, Pollak and Cohen 2005). Employment security
is particularly relevant in this study, as high rates of unemployment were reported
among the participants.

Loy's experience shows that many Asian immigrants, especially recent ones,
lack employment security:

> There were quite a lot of [Asian immigrants]. All the newly hired were terminated because of the slowdown in production. The other two that were hired together with me were terminated, including those who were hired earlier than we [were]. The company had reduced orders, so production slowed down.... I did not qualify for EI because I did not [have] enough hours to qualify. I should have worked for six months in order to qualify.... We were given some compensation aside from our wages. And thereafter for every three months [we had worked], we were given fifty to sixty dollars a month.

As evidenced throughout this chapter and Chapter Three, casual and part-time jobs are the norm for Asian immigrants, especially for their first jobs in Canada. Most often, participants wanted full-time, not part-time jobs; however, most participants found it hard to obtain full-time work. It is clear that the majority of Asian immigrant workers in part-time jobs are not the stereotypical teenagers or full-time mothers/homemakers who want part-time work and do not need to support a family on the wages from that work.

Participants often had casual full-time jobs, meaning that the workers were considered casual by their employers even if working full-time hours. This type of work is both prevalent and precarious. Not only are casual workers denied extended benefits, but they are also very likely to experience lack of employment security, as hours can vary from week to week or seasonally. Casual workers are also more susceptible to layoff and termination.

As noted earlier, the prevalence of part-time and casual jobs required several participants to hold more than one job at a time. However, people with two part-time jobs often end up dedicating more of their time to work-related activities than someone with a regular full-time job does. For example, the travel time between jobs must be considered as time that workers dedicate to work. Further, part-time workers can work thirty or more hours a week at one job and then the same at another — well over full-time hours but without the benefits that can accompany them. Participants can be overworked not only on a weekly basis, but also on a daily basis, as those with two part-time jobs often work far more than eight hours a day. In short, holding two part-time jobs is an undesirable alternative to full-time work.

Casual full-time jobs are quite common in the care aide professions — work taken on by many recent Filipino immigrants, especially women and former live-in caregivers. This kind of work is also often "split shift," meaning that two or more short shifts are scheduled with several hours between them, especially if it involves home care visits. One participant, Joy, articulated clearly that split shifts can often mean a very long work day:

> You have to commute. It is not a straight time. You have a time gap to transfer to another client. For instance, the schedule would be from eight to nine a.m., and then the next one would be from one to two p.m.... Sometimes [I meet] four [clients].... I am not paid for those

in-between hours. I only get paid for the hours that I worked for the patient. The travel time is not paid. If you have your own car, they give you mileage. If you don't have a car, you have to spend your own money.... For me, it is tiring. But I am enjoying my work. In the first place, I like taking care of older folks. When I see them after their bath or having been cleaned up, I feel happy for them. But of course, the travel time especially is sometimes tiring.... What do I do [between clients]? I just walk or stay in a mall while waiting. Sometimes, if the interval is longer, I call up my husband to pick me up, and I go home because there is enough time.

Not only was Joy unable to use her time off work to do as she pleased, she also had a very long work day. However, the very long work day often did not result in her being paid for even eight hours.

The survey results reported in Chapter Three showed that care aide work was the most common job for live-in caregivers to move into after meeting their residency requirements. On a superficial level, care aide work seems like upward occupational mobility, but it is not as significant as it seems. Rather, care aide work too often represents a transition from "pushing a stroller" to "pushing a wheelchair" — from dealing with children to dealing with the elderly and people with physical and mental challenges. Joy's story provides evidence of this:

It is not really eight hours. Sometimes when I attend to four patients, I am only six hours. Sometimes it is only five hours. Sometimes the company only gives you one hour for a client. Every client is not necessarily for two hours' work. There are some who are only assigned one hour. You just do personal care. You cannot do much in an hour. And then you move to the next client in another place. And sometimes the interval is three hours. This is the time when I go home and then go to another client. This is what I do for C that pays fifteen dollars and fifty cents per hour.

Like Joy, many home-visiting care aides work in one client's home, then move on to another client's home. They are not paid for the in-between time or the travel time and end up having far longer work days with only eight or six or four hours' pay. The in-between time is considered time off even though there is usually not enough time between clients to go home and rest or engage in some other personal activity.

Rose's narration shows another example of what care aides can be asked to do: "I started there last October. I have to still count [my hours].... He is paying me cash only." As Rose's account suggests, some care aides are asked to accept payment in cash and not to record hours formally. However, an employee being paid in cash does not have a documented record of work-hours. The record of work-hours can be critical — for example, under the 2002 ESA, records were needed to prove that a worker had completed more than five hundred hours of work and thus qualified for more than a training wage.

Almost every participant's narrative mentions "job-hopping." This was especially true for the first few jobs in Canada. Many first jobs were very short, lasting just a few weeks or less. Job-hopping is related to both "push" and "pull" factors — the push of needing a job, any job, and the pull of wanting a job with benefits and job satisfaction. For example, some participants took up a job quickly, but also left quickly because the job was too physically demanding or dangerous. It was common for male participants to leave a job for these reasons. Sometimes a participant who left a job for a better one found the problems at the new job to be the same.

Some participants reported having arguments and disagreements with their employers. Interestingly, no participants reported being fired solely for doing a bad job or violating policy. There was always more to the story than that, and it usually involved violations of workers' rights and the participant complaining about the violations. For example, Rose tried to get her employer to live up to the nine hundred dollars per month salary contract they had signed. Her employer told her that she did not need her services any more.

Many participants stayed in a job that was not secure and did not complain to the employer rather than risk losing their job altogether. Ronnie's narration below is an example of a participant coping with job insecurity.

> There is none [security]. And even if you are working, you can be terminated anytime. There is no security there as well. If they see that you are not very productive, they can just fire you. They just give you a two-week notice. In my work, I know some people in management, and I think they are quite satisfied with my work. My work is really very basic. You don't use your brain very much. Nor is there much skill. All you need is muscle power.

Job Security: The Effects of Discrimination

Since job security encompasses equal opportunities, discrimination is a major barrier to those who experience it. Although the questionnaire did not incorporate questions about discrimination, the testimonies of the Asian immigrants revealed many examples of multi-faceted discrimination. Tara described the discrimination she had experienced: "Yes, you can feel that people do discriminate against you, sometimes for your religion and at times due to your colour or race. Especially people discriminate on the basis of religion." Discrimination that the participants experienced was based on race, religion, dress, country of origin, and, in one case, transgender. Taqdees eloquently narrated her experience:

> I used to wear *shalwar kameez* [South Asian dress for some women], [but] the director of the institute advised me that if you keep on like this, you will not get any jobs. I will tell you the truth now, that I did not like her advice. I felt [bad about] it. I thought, why will I not

get a job, why is she saying this? Anyway, I learnt my lesson when I came into the practical field. I stood second in my diploma group, and everyone in my group, even those whites who did not pass the course, got jobs, but I didn't get a job. I kept applying for other jobs, and I went for one interview. I guess I appeared in two interviews at that time. I applied to so many places, but never got an interview call. During one interview the interviewer asked me a question that I can't forget. He asked me, "How long have you been in Canada?" I said, "Two years," and he said, "But you didn't adopt [Canadian practices] yet!" I didn't understand what he meant. I was wearing a head scarf at that time.

The above testimonies reveal severe discrimination in the form of racism and Islamophobia. In one case, the participant even discarded her veil just to get a job, and that decision eventually affected her mental health.

Job security entails the reasonable expectation for upward mobility as well as job satisfaction. While the International Labour Organization found a strong correlation between level of education and upward occupational mobility, this was not the case for most of the Asian participants. Fatima came into Canada with a PhD, but her experience contradicts the ILO's findings:

They never even called me for the interview. [They] just said you will have to revise and come again. Even when I applied as a volunteer in the hospital, they did not take me, saying, "your accent is different." Now I am seeing people with worse accents working.… They just refused. When [the hospital] called me for the interview, they said we have old citizens here, and you will have problems to communicate. I had worked in the [United] States for three years, but nobody had pointed that out there. So, I got disappointment continuously, whether I applied for a job, or a course, or volunteer work.… My degree was more than three years old, I had completed my PhD in 1995 … but they said we are only looking at your FSc./HSSC [twelfth grade] courses. They did not consider my PhD, only talked about my HSSC, and asked me to go back and study again.

Another participant, Mubeena, arrived in Canada with a positive mindset. She was confident that her transition to Canada from her country of origin would be easy and that she would find a career in Canada that was similar to the one she had pursued in her home country. However, living in the unpleasant realities of Canada, Mubeena's confidence decreased over time: "We had a totally different picture in mind, that there will be well paid jobs … and stuff, but when we landed here, we were taken by surprise looking at the job market situation here. And it was a great social and psychological shock too." Mubeena's degree from her country of origin was not recognized in the universities and colleges in Canada, requiring her to "start from scratch." Like many other immigrants, she found that every job demanded

"Canadian work experience" and/or "Canadian educational experience." Mubeena's initial self-confidence declined as a result of continuous negative feedback after she arrived in Canada. To make matters worse, Mubeena's husband, an electrical engineer, could only find a job as a vacuum-cleaner salesperson. Being in financial crisis and receiving no subsidy from the government, their first priority was to find any source of income in order to survive, then to pursue their educational ambitions. For a short time, Mubeena attended an institute; however, with the pressure of raising three children, she did not continue. Both Mubeena and her husband had to compromise their ambitions for the sake of raising their children as daycare was too expensive for them to afford.

By the time she applied to a call centre, Mubeena's attitude had completely changed. She had become doubtful, unsure of herself, and desperate. Mubeena landed the position, but taking it had a negative impact on her other career possibilities. Regardless of the difficult times they were experiencing, Mubeena and her husband did not ask for familial help. In fact, sometimes they lied about their lifestyle in order to "maintain a position in the family." Unfortunately, as many participants reported, it is difficult for an immigrant to land a job in Canada, especially a first job, without the aid of personal connections. Luckily, through her colleague's network, Mubeena later obtained a position as a financial advisor. Currently, she is a senior advisor for her employer. Although she has found decent work, Mubeena is not satisfied and wishes to pursue her career further, perhaps working for Revenue Canada or as an urban planner. She said, "I am making almost the same kind of money, but I am not internally satisfied. I think even after so much time, that lack of internal self-esteem is still there."

Skills Security: How Skills Advancement Gets Compromised

Training for skills advancement is offered by workplaces in which occupational mobility is possible, but such training was rare in the participants' workplaces. The majority of participants did not secure jobs in the areas in which they were trained, but rather found jobs that required little skill and had very little opportunity for significant occupational and professional advancement, for example in small restaurants or grocery stores. Since skills training is related to whether there are opportunities for advancement in a workplace, few participants received skills training. In other words, low-skilled jobs maintained a trend of downward occupational mobility for most participants.

Bong was one of the few participants who was successful in securing a job in the field in which he was professionally trained. He worked in an engineering firm that paid a part of the tuition fees for courses related to the job:

> They have a good program. If, for instance, you want to take a course, they give you a certain amount per year for your course. The company pays for a certain amount of your course.… Not yet. Maybe next year.

I plan to take a course. The company might pay for 50 percent, but you have to pass the course. Otherwise, you have to pay it yourself.… Let's say in electronics. You may want to take up one subject. Of course, you cannot take it full-time.

Even though Bong had access to courses subsidized by his employer, it is clear that he hesitated to take a course because he was afraid of the consequences of failing. For one thing, he would have to pay the total cost of the course himself if he failed. Bong's narration describes a situation where cost and fear of failure discourage an immigrant from upgrading — an important criterion for skills security.

Noel took a course at his own expense, but during the time he was taking it, he succeeded in getting employment that was closer to his original profession:

So far, yes. I have my personal satisfaction. Unlike my previous job, this one now is really along the line of my training and profession. Before, I would come home with cuts because I was working with glass, and my wife would tell me that I am not really destined for that type of job.… I did it because when I was doing production work, I wanted to improve myself and my job prospects. I did not want to be a production worker all the time. This is why I studied AutoCAD. I talked to someone who encouraged me to take this course. This guy was from an engineering company. But then, while studying, I got this present job as a warehouse supervisor. This job is in line with my former work in logistics.

Many participants reported seeking out upgrading or retraining or intending to do so on their own in the future. The intention to upgrade skills was almost exclusively related to the desire to work in the field in which a participant had been trained in the country of origin. Some participants accessed government-funded support, and some took out loans:

Rose: The government paid for this.… You see, I was not on EI. I was still working. I took the grant. They gave me $17,000 for the two courses.… from the BC Study Grant. It is actually a student loan.… Actually, I did not start it yet because I do not have any job yet, right? So, I applied for an interest relief program. But now, they have been calling me. I think I will have to start paying monthly.… I don't have to pay all of it.… But [the BC Grant] will pay 70 percent of this loan. So, I will be paying only 30 percent.… But then, the problem is, here in [this city], if you graduated from college here, you are given the priority. Another thing too, if you know somebody there, then you get a better chance of getting hired.… Well, the system.… it still counts whom you know.

Lila: I went to … college.… It took me a little over five months. I was able to pass the English exams. If I had not passed the English exams, it would have taken me a longer time because I would have to go to ESL, and it would have taken me around eight months to finish my studies.… I studied for nurse's aide full-time. I took out a student loan. I am still paying for this student loan. The loan cost me around $5,000. At the same time, I have been sending money to my daughter in the Philippines.

The above accounts illustrate that many Asian immigrants pay much, if not all, of the financial costs involved in upgrading and retraining. There is no doubt that these costs, along with the need to support family members in Canada and in the country of origin during re-training, hinder many Asian immigrants from achieving skills security and reproduce racialization and concentration in low-wage sectors in the labour market.

Representation and Voice Security: Unionization and Asian Immigrants

Representation and voice security involves certain aspects of global governance and national governance, and according to the International Labour Organization (2004: 338) it should also involve "a multitude of types of collective organization, to ensure that all legitimate interests in society can be heard effectively." The ILO explores emerging corporate social responsibility and points out that companies should not be expected to be responsible for social policy. This indicates that government should be accountable for social policy. The ILO further argues (2004: 334) that "a society in which basic economic security is regarded as a *right* requires that the values of social solidarity are at the forefront of policy." The preceding sections of this chapter clearly indicate that representation and voice security is lacking for most Asian immigrants. This lack may be one of the greatest barriers towards economic security, as each Asian immigrant's encounter in the workplace is individualized, personalized, and isolated, which eventually reproduces and sustains a racialized and marginalized workforce.

The narrations indicated that unionization is a significant determinant in the economic security of Asian immigrants. However, some participants had difficulties in getting protection and benefits despite their workplace being unionized. Several participants noted that new workers could not join the union until they had reached a seniority threshold of hours and were thus not protected from termination. For example, one participant was terminated despite his workplace being unionized because he had not yet met the six-month requirement.

Loy: The orders slow down in the winter because there is not much construction going on.… Yes. There is a union. But I have not filed for membership yet because I have not been there for six months. I would have been able to qualify for union membership had I been able to stay there for six months.… I don't think so. We were told that we could become union members only after six months. Only the older employers have unions.… There were quite a number of us who were laid off. We were all newly hired. Those of us who were laid off were basically temporary workers. And the hard work was given to us. The regular and permanent workers were doing mostly the spacers' work. It is relatively lighter than what we temporary or newly hired workers were doing. And once these people are done with the work on spacers, they don't have any more work except to clean up their spaces.

The *Employment Standards Act* formerly extended to unions, in the sense that a collective agreement between a union and employer could not establish standards below those in the Act. Now, however, with the 2002 changes to the ESA, the standards in the Act can be overridden by a collective agreement. Employers can now push for collective agreements that provide workers with lower standards than those outlined in the Act, and if weak, employer-led unions agree, the Employment Standards Branch cannot intervene to protect workers by insisting that the standards in the legislation be upheld. Surely it makes no sense to call the provisions in the Act employment "standards" if every workplace is not required to abide by them.

> Nenit: I only get EI and CPP benefits. The rest I have to pay for myself. My contract is that I work there part-time. We have a union, but it is not strong and the members are afraid to lose their jobs. And the union hardly speaks for the members. I think it is a "C" union [a weak union]. I also worked there as data entry operator. You have to accept whatever job they give you. After working there for eight months, I started looking for another job. This was also after I finished with my studies in computers.

Despite the change to the *Employment Standards Act*, unionization can lead to higher wages, job security, employment security, and so on, and all participants recognized the potential benefits and security of being a union member. However, even unionized workplaces do not provide security for all workers unless one becomes a member of the union and has passed the probationary period. As the narrations above and the one below demonstrate, Asian immigrants who work for a unionized company cannot take for granted that they can or will join the union and that their work situation will become more formal, standard, and secure.

> Joy: At B, I worked from Monday to Friday. It is regular, but I am only on call.... Right. It's like a casual job.... I am guaranteed at least thirty hours a week at B.... It is really more than thirty hours if I wanted to do more work. But it still depends on the call. My experience has always been that it has never been below thirty hours.... Their rate is thirteen dollars per hour.... At C it is fifteen dollars fifty cents.... Because C is unionized.

Furthermore, many Asian immigrants work in jobs that are not unionized. For this reason alone, many Asian immigrants lack voice and representation security in the workplace. Fatima eloquently summed up the situation for many Asian immigrant workers in Canada: "We are few in number, and there is no representative of our culture. Nobody raises a voice on our behalf."

Summary

Through Asian immigrants' testimonies, this chapter examined dimensions of seven levels of security in their lives. It is evident that various dimensions of security have been compromised in ways that perpetuate the production and reproduction of a racialized workforce of Asian immigrants in the lower echelons of society. A lack of unionized jobs among Asian immigrants further compromises their security in the workplace, denying them representation and voice. The significance of a union is that it facilitates Asian immigrants' collective representation. "Work security," the ILO's other key concept, is also significant for workers irrespective of race, gender, ethnicity, and nationality, and will be examined in the next chapter.

Notes

1. One participant used the term "husband." This term is not gender neutral, and I have used this term consciously to represent this woman's voice.
2. Immigrants to Canada enter under four broad categories: independent/economic, family, entrepreneurial or business, and refugee. Since the beginning of the twenty-first century, skilled immigrants are preferred in Canada. Currently, the majority of immigrants enter under the skilled/independent category.
3. In a welfare state, the government plays a key role in protecting and advancing the well-being and quality of life of the country's residents. The ideology of the welfare state recognizes that all citizens have a right to a decent quality of life, and therefore wealth redistribution, primarily through taxation, is essential. In a welfare state, the general population assumes responsibility for the common good of all. Because taxation is an important part of the mechanism by which the government can redistribute wealth (for example, through support for health care, education, employment insurance, and pensions), working conditions that encourage under-the-table payments run counter to the ideology of the welfare state.
4. Established in BC in 1973, S.U.C.C.E.S.S. is a multi-service agency. The mandate of the agency is to promote the well-being of all Canadians and immigrants and to deliver services in five major areas including employment, training, and education.
5. At the time of the survey, a caregiver who entered Canada under the federal government's Live-in Caregiver Program (LCP) was required to work and live at an employer's house for at least twenty-four months within thirty-six months. On April 2010, this changed to twenty-four months within four years, or for a minimum of twenty-two months if the caregiver has worked 3,900 hours. For details of the LCP, please see Pratt 1999; Bakan and Stasiulis 1997; Citizenship and Immigration Canada 2011 "Processing Live-in Care-givers in Canada" at <cic.gc.ca/English/resources/manuals/ip/ip04-eng.pdf>.

6.   A domestic worker comes under the LCP. Generally, the concepts "domestic worker," "caregiver," and "nanny" are used interchangeably although they can have numerous connotations.

7.   In Canada, major policy-oriented publications on immigrants have been done by the Metropolis project. The Metropolis project is an international network of academics/ researchers for comparative research on migration, diversity, and immigration integration and settlement in Canada and around the world. Funded by the federal government of Canada as well as provincial governments and associated universities, Metropolis BC (one of five national offices in Canada) was established in 1996 and is located at Simon Fraser University and the University of British Columbia.

Chapter 5

Work Security

Deregulated Work Sustains Workplace Hazards

This chapter uses Asian immigrants' narratives to examine aspects of work security that enhance or jeopardize workplace environments. The participants' testimonies provide a comprehensive picture of how workplace hazards, violations, and deregulation due to neo-liberal social policies, including the *Employment Standards Act* (ESA), compromise the work security and daily lives of Asian immigrants. Restructuring of the ESA has created "flexibilization" of work and contributed to inhospitable work environments perpetuating work insecurity and deregulated work. The participant interviews also indicate the limitations of the *Occupational Health and Safety Regulations* under the *Workers Compensation Act* and the unhealthy and unsafe working conditions that can result when employers create working conditions on the edge of or in violation of what the regulations require.

The International Labour Organization (ILO) (2004: 165) defines work security as follows: "Work security is about working conditions that are safe and promote workers' well-being." Work security therefore includes occupational health and safety, and mental and emotional well-being, and is compromised by features such as stress, overwork, violence, and harassment in the workplace. With such legislation as the *Canada Labour Code*, the *British Columbia Workers Compensation Act*, and *Occupational Health and Safety Regulations*, it can be said that regulation plays a major role in ensuring work security in Canada. Detailed analysis of these regulations is beyond the scope of this chapter, but various regulations will be mentioned as they pertain to the participants' narrations.

The BC government's restructuring of the ESA and the cuts in the services offered by the Employment Standards Branch contribute to the transfer of risk from employers to employees. Work security has been undermined in two important ways. First, the increase in casual work caused by the reduction of hours that must be paid for on-call work (from four hours guaranteed, down to two hours) means that fewer employees have access to the benefits provided to full-time workers. This includes access to paid medical and extended health benefits. Second, casual, informal work has potential impacts on safety. Workers who are casual are less likely to be provided with orientations or have adequate mentoring regarding safety aspects of the job. They are also less likely to feel they have the job security to make a complaint or even to ask questions. This increases the likelihood of injuries and the threat of income loss.

Tremblay (2009: 146) suggests that "insecurity is related to the perception of risk and this perception may vary from one person to another and in different contexts." This chapter examines how these changes have resulted in perceived risks and workplace hazards for each participant. The participants' narrations showed that their work security had been compromised in multi-faceted ways, each examined in a section of this chapter: 1) duration of work; 2) workplace orientation; 3) rights training; 4) skills advancement; 5) upgrading; 6) health hazards and safety in the workplace; and 7) the inadequacy of the ESA in handling violations of workers' rights.

Duration of Work

As mentioned in Chapter Four, almost every participant's account showed evidence of "job-hopping," which indicates an absence of work security for Asian immigrants. This was especially true for their first few jobs in Canada after arriving from their country of origin. Many of these first jobs were very short because on arrival most new immigrants took any employment they could find. As they made contacts, re-trained, or sought jobs closer to their education and experience, most immigrant workers left these first jobs for others that were better in some way. In almost all cases, participants reported that they quietly quit a job that involved too much physical labour, pain, or stress rather than approaching the employer to resolve the issue. Again, for immigrants, "job-hopping" was an easy alternative if the BC economy was booming and scarcity of labour was a major concern for employers.

Workplace Orientation

Some participants did not receive any workplace orientation, and some were not even interviewed for their jobs. These participants thus had little opportunity to learn about the wages, benefits, safety orientations, and workplace environments before accepting the jobs. However, most participants did receive some form of workplace orientation. These orientations varied in terms of their quality and the topics covered. Most participants received an informal orientation, often from a co-worker rather than a manager or supervisor, and often with no reading or visual materials pertinent to safety and health hazards. This casual orientation signals either a lack of policy or a lack of policy enforcement in terms of worker training and security. Casual training by co-workers can leave workers susceptible to receiving incorrect information. This is especially a concern with regards to safety. Casual training also leaves workers susceptible to abuse and exploitation, since workers may not be aware of what duties are truly a part of their jobs, according to their job descriptions, and which duties they should not be asked to do. It is also clear that some places where Asian immigrants work do not even provide job descriptions.

As Glecy's recollections in Chapter Four illustrate, lack of a job description often results in being asked to do unexpected work. Regan was another participant who started his job right away without receiving a job description or any information about the ESA even though at that time employers were required to post employment standards. The nature of Regan's job changed after 9/11 when the company laid off people, and he was asked to do a cleaning job. Without a written job description to protect him, the nature of his job changed dramatically:

> After I gave my résumé, I started working right away. They did give me some papers, but I cannot remember any more what that was. We were paid every two weeks…. They do have supplies of gloves when we do our cleaning up. I would use them. The factory slowed down after 9/11, and they started laying off people. I replaced the cleaner, which was not supposed to be my work. I ended up cleaning eight floors.

Another participant, Ronnie, wasn't sure of the procedures to follow if she were injured. Ronnie's testimony reveals that she was not aware of her rights and she did not feel comfortable complaining about her working conditions in order to be able to work more comfortably: "You are not allowed to sit down while working. They watch you. You work standing up for the whole day. You only get to sit down during break time."

Some participants did receive workplace training that took several days, involved reading materials, and even involved testing knowledge after the training. For most participants, this orientation and training, whether formal or informal, pertained to the nature of their job duties — the tasks they were expected to perform and the standard to which they should perform them. Many did not receive training related to safety or hazards or even to rights and benefits in the workplace. Obviously, it is in the interests of employers to inform their employees about what they are expected to do to perform their job. The experience of most participants was that employers did not see the same benefits to informing their employees about their rights and safety in the workplace. Some participants noted that employers would not want to tell employees about their rights because it would be disadvantageous for the employer. Sometimes, participants asked about rights and safety issues themselves, on their own initiative, recognizing that their employers were not going to freely offer information critical to workers' safety and well-being. Other participants, like Ronnie, were afraid to ask, fearing that it might compromise their employment security or appear that they were complaining.

Jenny, a recent immigrant, acquired a job delivering pizza at night without knowing the streets of Vancouver. Her account points out that her lack of knowledge about her job and the fact that she worked alone not only affected her ability to do the job well but also made her physically vulnerable:

> All I had to do was to make deliveries. But it was also dangerous because I was not yet very familiar with the streets of Vancouver. The

> first time I went on delivery, the owner just gave me the keys to the car and asked me to deliver to this particular area. I did not know the area, and the customer had to wait for almost an hour. The food was cold by the time I arrived. [The customer] was very angry. Sometimes I would have customers who frightened me. As well, I would deliver to apartments that I didn't know. And sometimes, I would deliver to customers in hotels.

Jenny was unsafe: she was simultaneously driving and navigating in the dark, and she delivered pizza at night to apartments and hotels alone. Such fear and stress can have long-term impacts on physical and mental health. It is noteworthy that the changes made to the *Workers Compensation Act* in 2002 by the BC neo-liberal government, changes aimed at reducing costs to employers, severely limited the access to compensation for mental stress caused by working conditions (Blaikie 2002; WorkSafeBC 2012).

When workplace orientation was carried out by a co-worker, the onus for orientation shifted from the employer to the employee, and the result could be minimal training, as Noel explained: "They just buddy you up with someone who shows you how to do the work. That is all." Noel's experience indicates that the central issue from the employer's viewpoint is the nature of tasks an employee performs rather than workplace hazards and orientation. Informal orientation, especially by a co-worker without the help of a supervisor, often places workers in an ambiguous situation even regarding pay, as Sid's narration reveals: "They did not tell me anything. I ended up asking them. My husband's nephews and nieces told me not to ask. But I did ask on the second day of my work. I asked: 'How much is the hourly rate here?' They told me that it was eight dollar per hour. They said that there are also no benefits."

Many participants come from countries where labour rights are largely non-existent and an authoritarian regime is the norm. Lack of workplace orientation, required under BC's *Occupational and Safety Regulations*, can lead Asian workers into undesirable workplace environments that might have been the norm in countries of origin. Like Sid, these workers are extremely vulnerable, and many might not have the strength of character she did to ask basic questions about wages and benefits.

This study found that participants who received pay above the minimum wage or benefits such as medical coverage and vacation pay tolerated a number of workplace violations. Noel's account is an example:

> It is difficult to reach that place. So, they give us additional pay. It's just like an incentive. You see, the other people there just start at nine dollars per hour. People don't stay long in that company. You have to put on a suit and mask when you work. The fibreglass smells so much. And when you come home after work, the smell sticks to you and your [clothing]. So, even if you have the suit, you still smell after

work. I always take a bath after work upon arrival at home. I don't want the child to be affected by the smell of the fibreglass. And you are not sure if you brought with you some of the fibres. It is not good for the child.... Also, the Filipino workers there helped me understand the work. They were the ones who helped and trained me in the work there. But I cannot remember if the company ever gave me any orientation about the hazards in the workplace.

Additional pay worked as an incentive for Noel to stay in a workplace where health hazards were not only part of his daily life but also could have an indirect impact on his child if Noel's clothes carried any contaminants home from work.

Ethnicity clearly played a vital role in Noel's workplace, with other Filipinos providing orientation and management providing little orientation, if any. Noel's narration provides another example in which immigrant workers are under-informed, the role of the union is non-existent, and the responsibility for training, and therefore safety, is transferred from the employer to the employee.

Rights Training

Some participants felt that they were familiar with the *Employment Standards Act* (ESA), but many others said they were not really sure what it contained. The majority who were familiar with the ESA had obtained the information themselves. Even though it has not been a requirement since 2002 for employers to post the ESA, some still did. An interesting finding is that where the ESA was posted in the workplace, workers read it and asked questions.

Most participants did not receive orientation or training related to workers' rights. Again, some had the initiative to ask questions or find out on their own, but it was apparent that information was not given freely. Some participants became more educated about their rights after experiencing abuse or ESA violations. For example, as described earlier, Glecy became more aware of her rights when she found out that doing child care for someone other than her employer was not part of the work a live-in caregiver had to perform. Another example was Jenny, a transgender person who took her case to the Human Rights Commission after experiencing abuse in the workplace.

Yes. It was after two pay periods when [my employer] called me and said, "Jenny, this is not going to work. I don't want to hear so much gossip here about you." I think there were workers who were jealous and said that there should not be any transgender working in that restaurant. He told me about this. He said: "Jenny, I would like to talk to you. I know that you are a good worker. I think your transformation is not going to work in this restaurant. I received so many complaints." The complaint is that — what is going on in that restaurant. There is a transgender working there. And I am going to the guys' and girls' washroom. I asked him if he is sure about these complaints. He said that he is sure that some customers have complaints about this.... I told him that I respect whatever decision he wants to make. But I insisted that I did not do anything wrong. It is just about my sexual/gender transformation.... So I left and was hired at once by [another employer].... I started working at [the second place], then went to the Human Rights Commission.... I talked to [my new employer] about my experience at [the first restaurant]. He gave me a number to call and told me to file a complaint at the Human Rights Commission. I filed the complaint. I sent the records that I made about my conversation with the owner of [the restaurant]. It was complete. It recorded all the things that I did on that day prior to my firing. I explained everything to the Commission. They sent a copy of my record to [the employer]. It stated that I was emotionally hurt that I lost my job. The Human Rights Commission sent me a letter and asked me to identify the guy who discriminated against me.... The guy agreed to settle with me in July.... Yes. I still have the papers and he agreed not to discriminate when hiring people and [that he] should not fire people without cause. But he did this also to another worker who was a lesbian. He fired that worker because the other employees did not like her.... And I told this to the Human Rights Commission.... I did not expect that there would be a financial settlement. I just wanted to complain against discrimination. The Human Rights Commission wanted me to name the settlement amount. I was not prepared for this, so I requested to talk first to the Commission alone. I talked to the Commission and told them that I just wanted to be paid what was due to me, and the total would be around $5,000. The owner, G, said that he would not pay $5,000 and would fight with his own lawyer. The Commission told me that it would be expensive for me to fight this. G counter-offered that he would pay two month's salary — around $1,500. The Commission said that they understand that I suffered emotionally, but I should accept the offer and go on with my life. It is good that I learned something out of this incident. I said that I would accept the counter-offer, but I don't want to see the guy any more.

Jenny's experience of being fired without cause and without being paid her final wages because she was transgendered made her more aware of her rights, although it was actually her new employer who explained how her rights had been violated and motivated her to complain to the Human Rights Commission. In other words, Jenny was successful in pursuing her complaint because someone who both had knowledge of the ESA and human rights and was in an authoritative position guided her, not because she was initially informed and aware of her workplace rights. Jenny's narration is another example of how vulnerable Asian immigrants are in the workplace and also suggests that transgendered people, gay men, and lesbians are also more vulnerable to rights abuse.

Skills Advancement

Training for skills advancement was offered by workplaces where there was the opportunity for occupational mobility — in other words, it was a rarity among the participants' workplaces. For example, Bong worked in an engineering firm that paid a part of the tuition fees for courses related to employees' work. As discussed in Chapter Four, Bong was one of the few participants who was successful in securing a job in Canada in the area in which he had been trained. The majority of participants did not secure jobs in the areas in which they had been trained, but instead found jobs that required little skill in workplaces with very little opportunity for significant advancement, like small restaurants or grocery stores. Skills training is related to whether there are opportunities for advancement in the workplace. In other words, unskilled jobs maintain a trend of downward occupational mobility. The following narrative reveals how Mubeena, an engineer in her country of origin, found her skills not advanced but rather eroded while working at her first job in the Canadian labour market:

> To be honest, I was so desperate for a job that I wouldn't have minded any job anywhere. And I just jumped into the opportunity that I got. I had no information on the company and what would be the job that I would be offered, but I was ready for it. They told me it was a marketing job. I came to know about all this during my interview. There was an opening, an opportunity, and I grabbed it. It was very tough and challenging. We came across a lot of hurdles as it was a marketing-oriented job, and they used to market in America through telemarketing. We had to meet targets. It was very stressful, but it gave me the strength to work under pressure. There was a sales target every fifteen days, and if you did not meet it, they fired you like crazy. One has to have strong nerves for that kind of job. We only used to get Sundays off. Sometimes they asked us to stay longer just to meet the targets.... It is a dilemma, what I am going through. I worked for N, got the experience, and also went for some basic education from B relevant to my studies in [my country of origin]. Now, wherever I go, they take my call centre experience as a negative aspect. I am stuck with that and now having problems in finding jobs in other sectors.... Then ... I applied to G and got a job.... This was through my colleagues' and friends' networks.... In these three years I have been promoted ... so I am a senior advisor over here. In the beginning, I was a financial advisor in the Collection Department, [but] later this department was closed.... I guess five to six years in this industry is more than enough and I feel like changing my job now. I am desperate to get into any government-related job. Like Revenue Canada. There are so many call centres, even in the Passport Office. So, I am serious to prepare myself for that [government] exam and change my job.

Mubeena's story reveals that her telemarketing job had negative effects on her résumé. None of her employers gave her training or upgrading for skills advancement. Mubeena acquired skills on the job, not through training or attending workshops, and she funded additional education herself. After serving five to six years in a number of jobs, Mubeena was eager to find a job with the federal government. She realized that her work experience would not be counted for the federal job, and she would have to write and pass the required exams. Mubeena's story confirms that for some Asian immigrants it is the employee, not the employer, who is responsible for skills advancement. Further, absence of skills advancement and training leads to work insecurity in the workplace.

Upgrading

Like Mubeena, many participants sought out upgrading and retraining on their own. The intention to upgrade skills almost exclusively related to the desire to work in the field in which participants had been trained in their country of origin or elsewhere. Some participants re-skilled themselves by taking courses or training from Canadian institutions. Some participants took out loans or used government-funded support. In all cases, upgrading happened as a result of an individual's effort rather than an employer's program. The following two accounts from Bade and Sofia demonstrate this point:

> Bade: I am working in a federal government's department.... I am applying for a different, higher position because this is still an entry-level job, and I plan to be in a better, higher level.... In the federal government, you have a lot of opportunities. There are a couple of good reasons to stick to this job: 1) stability; 2) good salary; 3) [benefits], and 4) many opportunities.... I told you that I completed from B [a course in] network administration. Since then I have developed a very good understanding of database. At N, I was working as a database administrator. [Currently] I am not working as a database administrator. So I want to apply to those positions where I will be able to work in database.... I think this will be a better paying job too.

> Sofia: I started volunteer work.... I decided before writing my exam I should take up clinical internship or something. I was aware that I will not be able to practise as a licensed doctor unless I write my exam. I came to know about this through the Internet.... I have to pass one more exam, the qualifying exam. And after that I will apply for residency. Basically, after passing the evaluation exam, they consider you as a doctor and it means that you did your medical studies.... After passing the exam you apply [for] the seats for immigrant doctors, and the Canadian-born will have more chances. The seats for immigrants are like thirteen to twenty seats, and the regular seats I don't remember right now. I think like the total seats available for immigrants are about

5 to 10 percent. It is much harder to get a residency in British Columbia as they say the living conditions here are better, and everyone wants to be here. I think the seats other than BC are more in percentage.... I think I was very lucky that I got this exposure. I live downtown. I went to a couple of doctors, but they were not taking any clinical trainees. I was able to get it because I was able to see Dr. N.... I met her through some friends.... Dealing with patients is entirely different. It is not easy to transfer book knowledge to practical practice. It is very important to have that kind of a clinical exposure. It is not all that easy for a lot of people. I don't drive; I take the bus then a sky train. It is like about a one hour and thirty minute drive one side. I come here only twice a week. But if I would have had something closer to my house, it would have been more punctual and frequent. I have my own house; my husband works there.

The above two narrations demonstrate that like skills advancement, upgrading is an individual effort for many immigrants. To re-skill, Bade went to Canadian educational institutions, worked in a call centre, and then landed a federal government job which provides her with better work security. She aspired to work in a database system where she could use her skills. Bade is typical of many Asian immigrants in having a very positive attitude towards federal jobs even though getting these jobs is very challenging. However, research has found that when racialized immigrants have finally passed all sorts of exams, both written and oral, their age becomes a major barrier to getting a federal government job — the "chicken-egg" dilemma (Zaman 2006).

Sofia, a medical doctor in her country of origin, migrated to Canada where her husband had a well-paid job. Because of her financial security, Sofia was able to upgrade her skills by writing and passing all the required medical exams. As well, she volunteered with a well-recognized institution to gain experience working under a Canadian doctor's supervision. Sofia's narration clearly demonstrates two points: 1) with financial security an Asian heterosexual woman can upgrade her skills and re-enter her original profession; 2) again, personal networking plays a vital role in terms of working in professional jobs such as engineering, medicine, computers and technology, nursing, and teaching, which ensure better work security.

Both Bade's and Sofia's accounts indicate that upgrading skills is a personal initiative and generally does not happen through the workplace or the employer's initiative. Unlike Sofia, however, most Asian workers, especially women, do not have the opportunity to upgrade and move to a workplace that enhances their work security.

Health Hazards and Safety in the Workplace

The interviews provided a great deal of evidence that participants worked in unhealthy and hazardous work environments. The problems included being the victim of unwanted and terrifying sexual advances, to the use of dangerous machinery, to exposure to hazardous chemicals, to working alone at night, to being required to stand all day. Some participants were not provided with protective gear like masks or hard hats, and participants working with chemicals did not always receive WHMIS (Workplace Hazardous Materials Information System) training or safe-lifting training. Most participants worried about the risks at these workplaces, but usually quit the job rather than complain.

The *Occupational Health and Safety Regulations* in BC clearly require that all employers, no matter the type of work or the number of employees, give their new employees orientations regarding health and safety in their workplace. Despite this requirement, participants often reported inadequate training. Ronnie's work situation is an example:

> I think I lift up to ... they are quite big. I think I would lift up to twenty-two to twenty-five pounds and sometimes up to forty pounds. If it is too heavy, we would ask the men to lift it for us.... They tell us to be careful with our backs.... None [no video or information session]. They just tell us to be careful, especially when doing lifting.

Ronnie did heavy lifting without sufficient training. In the case of especially heavy lifting, Ronnie was expected to ask for help from a male, most probably from a worker from her country of origin. There is no doubt that this kind of informal arrangement jeopardizes workers' safety.

Workplaces in the services and production sectors are often hazardous, and participants who worked in such conditions in privately owned enterprises frequently were not given the training or protective gear they needed to stay safe. William found that despite the obvious hazards at his job, his training was only related to how to make accurate cuttings, not to rights, safety, or health hazards:

> Not really [any health and safety training]. They just tell you of the specific that you are supposed to do. When it comes to safety, it is all up to you. There is also no training. Not training in the handling of equipment or machinery in the workplace.... They have a machine which is electrically operated. We cut them crosswise and by feet in terms of length. We make the measurement — where you have to be specific and accurate. Otherwise, if there is, say, a difference or margin of 1/8 of an inch, it would not fit. The cutting will not be accurate. The cutter is like a manual cutter. But it is hydraulic-pressured and you have to do it by foot.... None [No training].

It was surprising to find that while many participants complained of health ailments from the workplace, like bruises, sore backs, etc., none had suffered a serious injury, reported an injury, or made a claim to the Workers Compensation Board (renamed WorkSafe BC in 2005). However, participants were often told to report an injury to the employer right away, and the employer would offer them "deals" if they did not officially report the injury. This makes sense from the employers' perspective since injured workers can cost a workplace a lot of money in their dealings with WCB/WorkSafeBC.

While legislation regarding standards and occupational health and safety can be significant safeguards, the regulations, even if adhered to, are far from closing the loopholes on dangerous or unhealthy work situations. Edgardo's experiences illustrate this point: "I was in pain because of the long hours of work. You are standing all the time. When I was working at the greenhouse, it was my whole body that was in pain. But here in my work, it is my feet that are suffering."

Joseph's story also demonstrates the type of working conditions that many of the skilled Asian immigrants in the study worked in — low paying, unhealthy, unsafe, and extremely uncomfortable.

> They would give me around thirty-six hours of work per week. [Earlier] I would have received a cheque for over $300 a week. Now, I am only getting around $100 a week. They don't give me enough time. And when they give a shift time, it is mostly in the evening, and I don't usually take it. It is ok to work at night if you have a car. You can work outdoors. You can use the car while working outdoors. After thirty minutes outdoors, you can go inside your car and warm yourself up. But if you have no car, you have to endure the cold outside. Sometimes, after your patrol [outdoors], you can go to a corner of the building, but you still have to suffer the outside temperature, which is very cold. And sometimes the temperature goes down to minus one degree C.... We had to stay outside [at another work site]. Then, after our patrol, we had to go to the tent for a rest. But the tent is also open, and there is no heater in the tent. So, it is very cold. I finally refused the assignment.... They did not tell us [about the working conditions]. So, I reasoned out with them that this job assignment is too risky for me. This would cause problems for me if I am continuously exposed to this kind of weather outside. They understood this. But of course, once they pull you out, you have no more work. You have to wait for another assignment.... There is no guarantee of a forty-hour workweek in that company. You just have to wait for their call.... One time, here at L Plant, this company has a very clear policy that people working there should have reflectorized vests, hardhats, and steel-toed shoes. I explained this to the agency. You see, I was trained by L for one night about this. So when I started to report on Saturday and Sunday, I explained these requirements to the agency that I should have these safety gadgets to be able to work there as a security guard. But the agency insisted that I should just go there, that I am not going inside the plant, and I will be only securing the perimeter from outside the plant. Of course, because I needed money, I decided to work. But then, if anything had happened to me, or if there was any accident, L would be liable to the WCB or WorkSafe. Also, the agency, P, would be liable as well, and that includes me. Still, the agency insisted that I

would be outside the plant, so I can work without these safety gadgets. Fortunately, nothing happened…. But in places you are alone by yourself, there is no one there to replace you. You have to be creative to eat your lunch or take your break…. Basically, what they taught us is the basic standard training as a security officer. It is more about our work and responsibility. But we were not told of our rights as workers.

Joseph's working conditions, although unreasonable, were not in violation of the *Employment Standards Act*. If employers do not require uniforms, then they are not obligated to supply clothing, and workers are expected to supply their own steel-toed work boots. Regarding breaks, the ESA does not require that employees be given breaks, just that they be paid for working during what would normally be break times. The employer may have been in violation of the *Occupational Health and Safety Regulations*, which require that an assessment be done for severe temperatures. (In 2005 this was defined as temperatures that, including the wind-chill factor, were below minus seven degrees Celsius.) There are also safety regulations that stipulate that workers who are alone must have regular contacts to ensure they are safe. Joseph complained to the company, but he did not ask WCB/WorkSafeBC to investigate; he dealt with the situation by quitting work at that site, with the result that he lost a large portion of his income.

Working alone at night is a common feature of jobs for Asian immigrants. Rose's narration illustrates that situation: "Yes. I am just quite by myself while the radio is playing, and I am cleaning. There is no boss. And if in the morning they have complaints about your cleaning, they will just call you up."

This study found that most unionized workplaces and health-care sectors such as hospitals and clinics were more particular about safety and training and did train employees for safety, handling chemicals, hazards, and so on when safety hazards were related to the workplace. Further, an inspector might routinely visit the workplace to keep the environment clean and safe. These testimonies demonstrate the findings:

> Ambrosio: Your co-workers and your supervisor really watch you on how you do your work. They see that you perform according to what is expected of you…. They are quite fair. They don't get angry because you made a mistake. They just tell or remind you how to do things properly…. I learned how to work in a safe manner. For instance, before starting work you have to wear the necessary clothing so as not to contaminate the working place because the inspector also comes and inspects. You have to wear, for instance, gloves, hair nets, proper clothes, the correct shoes that are not slippery with steel toes. Your dress should be neat and proper, and you should be clean when you work because you are dealing with food that the store sells…. Yes. The supervisor trains and gives you instructions. Before I started working there, the supervisor walked me around the workplace and gave me safety instructions.

Edgardo: Yes [I received training]. At the N hospital. They told me to wait for their call. I think it was one of their supervisors who interviewed me. He manages the crew in that hospital. Then, they called you up for training, and you were paid. They showed you a video to demonstrate what to do. They also gave you an exam. Then, they hired you. This includes the handling of chemicals. But this is another department — the bio-hazard department.... I am assigned in housekeeping. They showed us how to do this. But they also included the training in bio-hazards. No. I was on call at that time. All of us who were on training at that time — we were assigned to different hospitals.

Another participant, Loy, found that workplaces varied in terms of handling chemicals, machinery, and glass. In one workplace, Loy was required to wear a mask and steel-toed shoes. In another place, she inhaled hazardous chemicals because she had no mask. Fear of losing the job silenced Loy, and she did not complain to WorkSafe BC:

I did have complaints.... They have safety glasses that we wear. We have also to wear steel-toed shoes.... We don't wear masks or anything for that matter. We do inhale the fumes of the glue. I did inhale the desiccant, which is a hazardous chemical. We only have glasses for our eyes. We don't wear any masks.... The previous worker whose job I took over was also not wearing a mask. But the other workers like the cutters and others use masks. They have uniforms that prevent them from getting injured if the glass they are working on breaks.... Yes, I did learn skills there. But I don't want to do it any more because I am worried about the job.... I think the chemicals are cancerous — especially the desiccant.... No. They did not tell us. But we can read about the chemicals because we are the ones using them. We would read the warning of the desiccant. It would say: "Hazardous and could cause cancer." We read this.... We would put them in the barrel. You see, there is a machine that sucks up the desiccant from the barrel. Once the barrel is empty, we have to fill this up so that the desiccant continues to flow. So what we do in the morning, we would start to load the barrel with desiccants that would last us until in the afternoon. The night shift would have to start doing the same after we leave.... We don't mix anything. We just pour the desiccant from the bag to the barrel so that the machine will be able to suck it up. With regards to butile, which is the glue, we would also load two packs of butile into the butile machine. Once the machine is empty, then I have to load it again. I have no one helping me out. I only wear gloves, but it is a thin glove — only to prevent dirt from sticking to you because the butile glue is dirty, and it sticks. And the spacers have to be kept clean; otherwise they would be rejected by the customer.... No, they did not show us anything. They just trained us and let us do the work at once.... I think so, except for the masks and jackets for glass. But

> even these are not enough as some are still injured…. The lead man would do first aid…. Yes. There was one time when the glasses were piled up. These are wide glasses, but thin individually. One of these glasses fell down, and one of the guys was hit by the glass [and had] splinters in his arm. The other one was hit on the head. There were two of them, both hit by glass splinters. If they were hit directly by the falling glass, they would have been killed. There was so much glass splinters…. They do have long sleeve jackets for protection. But when that glass fell down, they were hit by the splinters. I heard that there had been a lot of accidents…. Not in our department. The dangerous ones are really in the cutter department and the transfer of the glass…. Yes. People get cut, they get scratches, or because the glass is sometimes very clear, they cannot see it and hit it.

Loy's workplace environment was clearly dangerous, yet she and others continued working there without adequate protective gear and knowledge. It is impossible to predict the long-term impacts conditions like this could have on a worker's mental and physical health. Unless there is a major accident that causes death, such hazardous workplaces are generally beyond the purview of the media and go unreported.

Edgardo worked for forty and more hours a week at one job, but his work was considered casual. His job entailed handing very heavy containers down to other workers, and he did this job without safety restraints or safety training — another example of violations of the *Workers Compensation Act* in the workplace:

> I worked in the farm. It was a greenhouse mostly planted with tomatoes. This was in Richmond…. I was a picker, loader. I would unload lots of stuff. They were quite heavy. I am not used to that kind of work. There was not a day upon coming home that I would not have a back massage. I was in pain all over my body…. I worked eight hours a day. We had a break time of thirty minutes for lunch. We also had a coffee break in the morning. I was making only eight dollars [an] hour…. I was only working casual there…. I was working for five days and eight hours a day. Sometimes we worked for six days. So, more than forty hours sometimes…. I worked there for one month. But it was difficult for me…. No training. They just asked you to do things right away…. I was not sure of my steps at that time, and I was shaking because we were working above the ground…. The working area was quite high. You have to bring down the container loader from high above the ground, and you lower it down through the rope. It is quite heavy.

Work Insecurity, Complaints, and Coping

As the previous sections clearly indicate, this study found many cases of low wages and poor working conditions, as well as violations of workers' rights, both under the

Workers Compensation Act and the *Employments Standards Act.* Only in Jenny's case was the employer penalized, and the monetary amount the employer was required to pay was not what Jenny asked for. The majority of participants who experienced violations quit their jobs and did not report the violations.

Many participants mentioned that they were not really sure of their rights, especially when they first arrived in Canada. This left them susceptible to exploitation during their first and sometimes their subsequent jobs. Participants made this connection themselves, also noting that they were afraid to ask about their rights. Some participants knew their rights but did not try to enforce them. Possibly participants made some kind of "trade off." For example, they were happy to have wages and perhaps some benefits, so they did not want to complain and risk losing them. Edgardo articulated this very well: "I am not really interested [in my rights].... My other friends who work there were telling me that after having worked there for a while, they were getting bus passes." Several participants also noted that their employer did not or would not want them to know their rights, and some said that they had been discouraged from talking to their friends about the subject.

One of the major findings of this study is that no participant reported using the "Self-Help Kit." No wonder that complaints by workers dropped 60 percent over the first three years since the 2002 ESA changes (Fairey 2005). This is essentially the same phenomenon the Canadian Centre for Policy Alternatives found with welfare — the fact that there are fewer cases does not mean that people are moving into work (Cohen et al. 2006). In the case of Asian immigrants, certainly, fewer complaints do not mean that fewer workplaces are violating workers' rights. Workers are deterred from complaining for fear of losing their employment. And really, this may have been the whole point of the changes to the complaints processes in the first place. Most Asian immigrant workers were reluctant to complain. The new focus of the ESA on a complaints-based system did not protect them.

Most Asian immigrant workers simply do not complain except to their friends and family. Those who think of officially complaining encounter the kit, which in itself is designed to act as a deterrent. Use of the kit assumes that job security is not compromised by facing the employer and complaining. However, participants noted that job security was one of their biggest concerns. For this reason alone, employers in the sectors in which recent immigrants work almost exclusively "get away" with repeatedly violating workers' rights.

Most participants quit their jobs rather than make complaints about wages or working conditions. Edgardo was one who quit his job:

> What I found out was that there were many workers there who were also complaining, especially about the low wages. They don't [get a] raise, and if they get it, it takes a very long time. They are stuck at eight dollars seventy-five cents an hour. Some had been there for a long time, and they had not had any raise.... They could not because they are not unionized. And the working conditions are not very good.

Like most racialized workers, Joy's work situation was tenuous. Instead of quitting her job, Joy used a coping mechanism to help herself get through a challenging work situation:

> The first time I was assigned at A hospital, I did not know that the patient was confused, and he was hitting at people around him with his cane. So I asked the nurse and she explained to me what kind of patient this guy was — that he hits people with his cane. I did not know what to do because he was screaming, and he did not want to see you in front of him. If that is the status of the patient, all you have to do is redirect his attention, like show him some pictures. You have to distract him to get rid of his anger. If he calmed down, I would walk him around the hallway of the hospital. I just wanted him to spend his energy. Also, you don't want them to be in their bed all the time. Sometimes, he would tell me that he wanted ice cream, so I would go with him to the main floor where he could buy ice cream. That was really an interesting experience for me. I was still new at that time. [At first] I almost wanted to go home when he was confused.

As described earlier in this chapter, one of the most extreme examples from the interviews of the inadequacy of the ESA in handling violations of workers' rights was Jenny. Despite being abused in the workplace, fired without cause, and not being paid her final wages, Jenny went to the Human Rights Commission rather than using the "Self-Help Kit" or visiting the Employment Standards Branch. Her experience, and that of many other participants, confirmed that Asian immigrants complain only when it comes to wages. The combination of the workers' reluctance to complain, the limitations of the *Workers Compensation Act*, and the restructuring of the ESA is a dangerous one that can only result in Asian immigrants continuing to work in hazardous and substandard conditions.

Summary

It is evident from the interviews carried out for this study that most new and Asian immigrants do not know about the ESA or the WCA. The interviews also revealed that some participants knew their rights regarding employment standards and safety but did not try to enforce them. Possibly participants made some kind of "trade-off," feeling happy to have wages and benefits and not wanting to complain and risk losing them. Many participants noted that their employers did not or would not want them to know their rights. A number of workers' rights and ESA violations were apparent in participants' descriptions of their workplaces. In only one case was an employer punished and required to pay a financial penalty for violating a worker's rights. The majority of participants who had experienced violations or unsafe working conditions quit their jobs. These workers did not report violations and were reluctant to complain. The new focus of the ESA on a self-help, complaints-based system does not protect Asian immigrant workers. No participant reported using the "Self-Help Kit" made part of the 2002 revised ESA. All of these factors add up to a sobering fact: that little in the current, deregulated ESA or in the WCA stops unscrupulous employers in the sectors where so many recent and Asian immigrants work from continuing to violate workers' rights when economic security is at risk. The deregulated ESA also contributes to workplace hazards by helping to maintain an environment in which the fact that workers do have rights is invisible.

The next chapter illustrates how Asian immigrants exert their individual and collective agency in their struggles for basic security and decent work. Some participants attended a workshop to propose alternative policies to respond to the restructuring of the ESA. The next chapter outlines their proposals.

Chapter 6

Individual and Collective Agency

Intersections of Basic Security and Asian Immigrants' Lives

This chapter examines how Asian immigrants exert their individual and collective agency after migrating to Canada and how they struggle for basic security and decent work. Some participants of the survey attended a workshop organized by the Philippine Women Centre (PWC) and the Department of Women's Studies at Simon Fraser University to respond to the restructuring of the *Employment Standards Act* (ESA) and to propose alternative policies.[1] To explore individual and collective agency of Asian immigrants in dealing with basic security, this chapter has three sections. Individual agency is illustrated in section one through four women's life stories after migration to Canada. The role of the PWC is examined in section two because the centre illustrates collective agency in several ways: through its active role in collaborative research, including in this participatory research study; by upholding Filipino rights nationally and globally; by opposing the violation of rights and discrimination of all types; and by forming broad-based alliances for social justice.[2] In the final section of this chapter, the objectives, the range of participants, and the recommendations of the workshop pertinent to the restructuring of the ESA will be discussed.

Individual Agency

Through interviews, a number of participants exerted their individual agency and narrated their struggles and strategies after immigration, their aspirations, and their level of satisfaction or dissatisfaction with their economic security.

Saba: Hard Work Paves the Road to Economic Security

Saba shared her story which is woven with struggle, dedication, hard work, and success. In her country of origin, she was a notable teacher in biology, chemistry, and physics; she then migrated to Canada where she took a completely different and unexpected path, a route that is both challenging and inspirational to other immigrant women. In Canada, she attended a private college that unfortunately disappointed many of its students due to its financial difficulties, requiring Saba to broaden her horizon by attending a second college. Without much support from her family members in her country of origin, Saba was still motivated to learn and push herself further. Her husband's contributions and support provided her with

102

some strength to move forward. Regardless of driving herself and her family more into economic crisis, Saba still continued to quench her thirst for education and success. According to Saba, as an immigrant, her outward appearance was not easily accepted. However, she was not hesitant about asserting her identity as a veiled Muslim woman. Though she did not wish to isolate herself completely, she did not neglect her beliefs and values either.

Saba started in average-waged jobs and is now satisfied as an administrative assistant working for a federal government department. However, having reached this position does not stop her from continuing to move forward, something she advises all her fellow immigrants — both men and women — to emulate. She urges her people to move to their potential; to achieve in jobs other than cab driving or child care:

> The government should provide … similar jobs in accordance to [immigrants'] qualifications. The sooner the better; then, it will be more beneficial for them and the society.… Otherwise don't give them immigration if you think that they are not up to the mark. Because the government is not doing anything for the immigrants, most of them end up driving taxis or doing odd jobs.

Though Saba believes that racism is evident in Canadian society, she does not believe that racism is always a factor in employment. Instead, she believes that members from her own immigrant community fear to apply themselves and lack the confidence that is needed in order to survive as an immigrant. She shared her success, saying, "My strategy from the very beginning was that I want to prove myself. For this I had to work hard, harder than the other crowd."

Tara: A Versatile Woman Identifies Issues Recent Immigrants Encounter

Tara and her husband migrated to Canada in 2002 because of Canada's opportunities for immigrants and the well-being promised to the younger generations. Immediately upon arrival, Tara pursued her passion as a textile designer, but because of Canada's failure to "recognize or give value to [immigrant] degrees," Tara took a completely different path: she studied to become a pharmacy technician and nursing aid. Overall, her encounter with education as an immigrant has been negative. Tara said that even after spending time and money, her education does not guarantee that she will find a job, let alone a source of income security.

Tara is a very strong individual. Even in desperate times, she did not succumb to the low-wage jobs that are most pervasive among Asian immigrants. Unlike many skilled immigrants, she refused to be exploited and remained determined to continue her education, even though she viewed as "unfair" the lack of recognition of her existing education and the requirement that she obtain a Canadian qualification. In addition, not even discrimination stops her from achieving the best of her potential: her answer to discrimination is, "Who cares?" Along with being a versatile person, Tara is very successful in addressing certain types of discrimination that immigrants face, particularly in areas of volunteering:

> I applied for other jobs as well in the field of pharmacy but was unable to get a job. I even tried to get a job as a volunteer, but they did not even take me for a volunteer job. They said you should have experience. But they don't understand. If I am not given a chance, how will I gain experience?

Tara's story is one of courage, and she gives hope to other immigrants as she urges them to break away from the shackles of exploitation:

> The labour market of Canada is very good and progressive. But the new immigrants are being exploited. People work so hard and don't get proper [pay]. I think they should make the minimum pay as ten dollars an hour. Due to the price hike and all, I think they should increase the per hour rates. It is very hard to maintain the standard of living in comparison to what people have in [their country of origin]. The majority of the people have come from the middle or upper-middle classes. They have struggled there to achieve a standard, and after coming here, the struggle starts again. I think my standard of living has decreased after coming to Canada.

She argues that the problem is that many immigrants — because they are positioned in a financial crisis — are forced to work in low-wage and non-standard jobs, thus preventing them from applying for jobs that are suitable to their professions in their countries of origin. She recommends that immigrants not worry about having a source of income but rather educate themselves first. She has great faith in immigrants, claiming that they should not be mistaken as "illiterates." Though Tara offers excellent advice, skilled immigrants cannot let their families starve; consequently, they work in low-wage sectors and hazardous workplaces in order to make ends meet.

Fatima: Urging for Voice and Representation Security

Most Asian immigrants migrate to Canada in the hope that they will have a more prosperous future ahead of them. However, this was not the reason Fatima and her husband immigrated. Both had careers and many years of higher education in their country of origin. Fatima was an assistant professor of zoology in a university, and her husband was an electrical engineer. Both were privileged to have the opportunity to pursue their careers in America, leading Fatima to assume that Canada would also be welcoming. Fatima says, "We applied for immigration [in Canada], and we were of a point of view that both countries [Canada and the United States] will be the same." Her perception of America was also negative in some respects, however:

> The USA does not have a sound financing package. If you do not have a job, you will be on the streets. When you are on a job, you may get excellent rewards, but if they close the project, the financial position of the USA is not that sound to take care of their citizens. In comparison, the health benefits and financial security here in Canada is better. You have the social security here.

Even taking into account the United States' intolerable lack of social security, Canada seems to have failed Fatima and her husband more. Logic does not seem to cross from one border to another. Fatima is not hesitant to question why it was possible to achieve a good position in America and not in Canada. In Canada, her husband's income was reduced, and Fatima's employment was downgraded to a customer service representative working for N.

Like many other immigrants, Fatima and her husband migrated to Canada with great confidence. She said they thought, "We are talented with good education and will get suitable jobs according to our qualification." Her high confidence has decreased, leading her to refer to herself and her husband as "losers." Canada failed to recognize their qualifications, forcing them to start from the bottom and work their way up. This was not simple for a woman who constantly faced discrimination. Besides being refused employment and volunteer opportunities because of her "different" accent, she also faced other forms of discrimination because of her religious beliefs, belonging to the Islamic faith. She recounted the shocking experience she suffered while studying for her licensed practical nurse (LPN) qualification: she was the only student who failed even though she had the most knowledge in that area. She is critical of Canada, which fails to recognize "educated, responsible, capable, hard working" immigrants like herself:

> They don't want to change or lose their monopoly.... [There is] some discrimination against the people who have migrated from [my country of origin]. Because we are few in number, and there is no representative of ours, nobody raises a voice on our behalf.

Fatima concluded by offering advice to fellow immigrants. She suggested that they explore their opportunities and not waste time but rather grasp opportunities immediately before they slip from their hands. She finished with a powerful message: "Do not stay at home and do not keep quiet."

Nadia: An Immigrant Who Believes Goals Are Essential to Success

Nadia and her husband are both physicians in Canada, and thus they have a higher level of basic economic security than other immigrants who occupy low-paying, low-status, temporary, and non-standard jobs. In addition, their three children, who are Canadian-born, are in a better position to access the opportunities that Canada presents for the young, compared to older children who immigrated to Canada. However, regardless of her duty and dedication to her profession, Nadia emphasized that she is "a mother first and then ... a professional."

Having a comfortable level of economic security means that Nadia and her family have few complaints. When asked to reflect back on her arrival in Canada, Nadia was positive, saying, "The people were nice." Her complaints were very minor; she commented on Canada's bad weather, its snowy conditions, and the difficult transition in adjusting to different foods.

Because Nadia's husband was already a doctor in BC, she had access to information and to the profession when she migrated. She feels that she faced neither discrimination nor barriers upon studying to become a doctor. She said, "No, I did not [face any discrimination]; in fact, in this profession, people respect you irrespective of your background or whatever." While Nadia said that having a supportive husband prevented discrimination from occurring, she believes that goals are the most crucial element to achieving success:

> Well, the main objective is your goal; whatever the circumstances are, one should strive hard to achieve the goals, and if you do so, you can achieve what you desire. Having no one to guide [you] doesn't mean you cannot achieve it.

She said that, unlike many other immigrants, she did not give up. She was not reliant on her husband's aid because she had her mind on her goals. She said, "If you concentrate on your studies and realize that you have a bright future waiting ahead, you don't mind all this [depression]."

When asked, Naida did not comment on whether or not there is "discrimination or fears in the minds of the policy makers," but emphasized the need for practical experience in Canada.

> You need to do the residency program in this country. Bookish knowledge is very different when you come in contact with the real life situation; [when] you apply your knowledge, it is entirely different. The residency is very important as you are playing with somebody's life. If you think you come here and start working as a doctor it is very difficult. [Immigrants] have to come in contact with the patients; they have to have practical awareness.

When asked to describe which class[3] she belongs to, she responded:

> I am very very satisfied and happy. I have what I wanted, and I have it the way I wanted it. The good thing about my job is that I can adjust my timing; I am my own boss. This is the beauty of Canada, that once you have done whatever their requirements, and then you can adjust yourself according to your own.

When asked if she voices specific issues that Asian immigrants face, she said, "Not really. On the individual level we do talk to each other, but not as a forum we haven't." While not involving herself in activism or advocacy initiatives, as a privileged and skilled immigrant, Nadia said she makes sure to help her fellow immigrants.

An Example of Collective Agency: The Philippine Women Centre in BC

Established in 1990, the Philippine Women Centre (PWC), a non-profit society, operates at local, national, and global levels. In BC, the PWC is an active organization located in the Downtown Eastside in Vancouver. The PWC also has networks with Filipino groups in Victoria, Kelowna, and Kamloops and strives to connect to Filipino in even smaller towns in BC where live-in caregivers work. At the national level, the PWC has established centres in Toronto, Montreal, and Winnipeg during the past ten years. All these centres organize events, protest meetings, and demonstrations against racist and sexist immigration bills and policies, and against exploitative labour laws and practices in different provinces. At the global level, the PWC has strong links with Gabriela Philippines — the national alliance of militant women's organizations in the Philippines — the Gabriela Network in the US, MIGRANTE International, and so on. In addition to raising consciousness about the historical and transnational contexts of Filipino women's mass exodus from the Philippines, the PWC aims to advance and restore Filipino women workers' rights across provinces in Canada and beyond the border.

To protect the rights and dignity of Filipino immigrants and migrants in Canada, the PWC organizes various events throughout the year including consciousness-raising workshops, petition-signing, annual fund-raising dances, and participatory action research projects. One of the examples of the participatory action research projects is the PWC study, *Housing Needs Assessment of Filipino Domestic Workers* (1996), which eventually led to a collaborative project with SIKLAB, a migrant organization for Filipino workers. This collaborative project arranged affordable co-op housing for domestic workers who desperately needed this type of alternative arrangement. In assessing housing needs for marginalized Filipino workers, the PWC established alliances with groups such as the Tenants' Rights Action Coalition (TRAC), the Downtown Eastside Residents Association (DERA), and the Co-operative Housing Federation of BC. Further, the PWC conducted a community-based, action-oriented research project entitled *Canada: The New Frontier for Filipino Mail-Order Brides* (2000). This study exposed how Filipino women as "mail-order brides" migrate to remote areas in Canada and how this innovative migration process has intensified due to the global predatory forces.

Through its collaborative research with the Feminist Research, Education, Development and Action Centre (FREDA), the PWC also exposed the structural and systemic de-skilling of domestic workers in a study titled *Trapped: "Holding on to the Knife's Edge": Economic Violence Against Filipino Migrant/Immigrant Women* (1997). This study demonstrated the de-skilling of domestic workers who had been nurses, teachers, and midwives in the Philippines. This de-skilling was so pervasive that it was identified as economic and social violence. Compiling a number of recommendations at the provincial and federal levels, this study urged both levels of government to recognize immigrants' country-of-origin credentials, including education, training, and job experience. The study rightly pointed out that accreditation of immigrants' credentials would pave the way for immigrants' integration and settlement in Canada. Interestingly, this study was conducted before Canada's emphasis on the current skilled category immigration.

In 2010, the PWC celebrated twenty years of grassroots activism for the empowerment and liberation of Filipino women in Canada. The PWC news release[4] stated:

> We fight for all Canadian workers for fair working conditions and just wages. Yet workers' movements without a feminist perspective are fundamentally flawed, just as feminist movements without class consciousness and action are destined to falter. Thus, in challenging women's movements, economic organizations, and labour policies in Canada, we contribute to transforming society.

The above statement recognizes women's movements and labour movements in Canada by making links between feminism and class, and the PWC's own goal is to make intersections between class and feminism. Simultaneously, the PWC aspires to mobilize Filipino immigrant and migrant women to achieve basic security, i.e., decent work conditions and work security. Toward achieving this goal, the PWC, in 2010, celebrated the 100th International Women's Day in collaboration with many community groups including the Grassroots Women's group, a BC-based feminist and working-class organization.[5] As the PWC's inception was connected to Filipino women's mass migration and domestic workers' working conditions in Canada, it is not surprising that it has a very strong working-class base and builds alliances with grassroots organizations in BC such as the Aboriginal Women's Action Network, No One Is Illegal, East Vancouver Abolitionists, New Noise, Vancouver Rape Relief and Women's Shelter, Pakistan Action Network, Bolivia Solidarity Group, and so on. As a broad-based collective agency, the PWC has the potential for far-reaching social transformation relating to Asian immigrants' basic security.

Because of the collaboration with the PWC, under Cecilia Diocson's guidance it was possible to make contact with women who migrated to BC under the Live-in Caregiver Program and to understand the impact it has had on their lives. This was not an outcome originally anticipated. The PWC collaborated with Simon Fraser University and the Canadian Centre for Policy Alternatives in organizing the workshop described in the next section.

Participatory Research Generates Solutions
for Economic Insecurity of Recent Immigrants

Once the survey was completed and some intensive interviews were conducted, a workshop entitled "Asian Immigrants in BC: What do government policy changes mean for Asian immigrants in the labour market and what are the solutions?" was held on April 8, 2006. In addition to the Simon Fraser University Department of Women's Studies and the Philippine Women Centre in BC, the Canadian Centre for Policy Alternatives played a leading role in organizing this workshop (see Appendix 1). The workshop created a platform for the study and survey participants and community representatives to link individual and collective experience through collective analysis. This participatory action research model (PAR)[6] involves all parties relevant to the issues at hand in continual and active discussion, examination and reflection, which leads to ideas for social change. In other words, the PAR model is emancipatory, as participants who were mostly marginalized and racialized immigrant workers and researchers worked together to formulate policies for social change at federal, provincial, and local levels. The goal of the workshop was twofold: to explore the preliminary findings of the study and to develop alternative policies in response to the restructuring of the *Employment Standards Act*.

In all, over sixty people attended a day-long workshop. The participants included community members and participants from the interviews and survey, union representatives, academics, representatives from non-profit organizations/ immigrant groups, and representatives from the provincial and federal governments. The participants were asked to develop policy alternatives and solutions to the problems identified in the research, in keeping with the PAR model.

The workshop started off with a brief introduction, followed by an overview of the BC Liberal government's 2002 changes to labour market policies and legislation,[7] highlighting that while the government has argued that the changes removed "restrictions" in order to make the workplace more "flexible" for an increasingly competitive, global marketplace, the amendments ultimately removed protections for workers by reducing the enforcement role of the government and reducing benefits and the minimum wage for some workers — in fact, the already most vulnerable workers, recent immigrants.

Cecilia Diocson of the PWC presented the context of the research, highlighting the social, economic, and political background of Filipino migration as well as the issues confronting Filipino immigrants in Canadian society, where most face de-skilling, downward occupational mobility, and, frequently, notoriously bad working conditions.

The project's research assistant, Rebecca Scott, a student of SFU Women's Studies, then highlighted some of the preliminary findings from the survey component, showing the general demographic and socio-economic characteristics of the sample. Following this, I shared preliminary findings from the interviews, which showed that immigrants are experiencing increased insecurity since the labour market has been changed due to the restructuring of the ESA. I then made brief policy recommendations to get the next and most critical part of the workshop going, i.e., formulating alternative policies.

Participants were then broken into smaller groups of seven to ten people and asked to develop policy and program recommendations in the areas of working conditions, workers' rights, workers' supports, the role of unions, and so on. (Details of the discussion questions are in Appendix 2.) Moving from sharing their experiences, to analysis, to policy recommendations, each group had something new and innovative to add to a growing list of ideas aimed at increasing economic security for recent immigrants. Their recommendations showed the strength of the PAR model in working with grassroots groups to develop solutions that are more likely to succeed and be responsive to self-identified needs. Based on the preliminary findings and the recommendations of the workshop pertinent to alternative policies to the ESA, a report (print and online) entitled *Workplace Rights for Immigrants in BC: The Case of Filipino Workers* (Zaman, Diocson, and Scott 2007) was published. Once the report was published, several members of the news media interviewed us. The online version was downloaded approximately twenty thousand times in less than a year. This indicates that there is a high demand for knowledge about workplace rights for immigrants and, indeed, for all workers, in BC.

Participants' Recommendations: Policy Alternatives

- Get rid of the training wage. This is a ridiculously low wage. There are more benefits to paying a decent wage including worker loyalty and productivity.
- Raise the minimum wage to ten dollars per hour. This will pave the way to increased basic security for all workers irrespective of race, gender, and country of origin.
- Provide a written job description, including expectations and contracts, to the employee on hiring. This will eliminate confusion, stress, harassment, and overwork and will ultimately lead to work security.
- Make the schedule available to workers ahead of time. Stability in their schedule may help workers maintain another job when needed. In addition, such stability will assist workers in organizing their own personal and family life and ultimately strengthen their basic security.
- Post the *Employment Standards Act* in the workplace. This will increase work security. Workplace rights only have meaning if workers know about them and feel able to demand and exercise them. Otherwise, these are "paper rights" only. The language of the ESA should be accessible and in pamphlet format. To increase awareness, make the ESA available in places other than the workplace, such as bus stations, airports, community services, and so on.
- Provide information sessions for employees and employers on the ESA and workers' rights and make attendance mandatory. Since 2001, seven of the top ten immigrant-receiving countries are from Asia, and labour rights are almost

non-existent in many of these countries. These immigrants need to be made aware of their labour rights. The alternative is exploitation of immigrants.

- Institute more proactive monitoring teams like the Agricultural Compliance Team. A monitoring team will be able to locate hazardous workplaces where workers' rights are being violated or have the potential to be violated. Such a team could also protect employees against arbitrary and wrongful dismissal.

- Make the ESA apply to both unionized and non-unionized workers. It is the government's moral responsibility to protect all workers, whatever their status. Taking this step would secure proper representation in the workplace and provide basic security.

- Get rid of the "Self-Help Kit." It is a clumsy and complicated document, and hardly anyone uses it. If no one uses it, what purpose does it serve? Workers need immediate access to a third party to mediate a complaint. Replace the kit with a community-based and non-profit system, which will be tasked with investigating complaints.

- Institute higher penalties for contraventions, for example a point-penalty system, like driver's insurance. Higher penalties work as disincentives for contravention.

- Make safety monitoring mandatory. If an employer's company is larger than a certain size, safety orientation should be a requirement. Smaller workplaces should be required to have a risk assessment. This is one way to reduce workplace hazards and enhance work security.

- Create a stronger monitoring and enforcement system. Rights are not implemented effectively unless a strong monitoring system is enforced. Otherwise, employers will get away with not implementing workers' rights and these rights will be "paper rights" only.

- Pay workers for the shift for which they were originally scheduled.

- Extend the minimum hours to four. Two hours of pay is grossly inadequate in a metropolitan city where recent immigrants must take the bus to go to the workplace. This kind of employment security will enhance workers' productivity and loyalty in the workplace.

- Provide tax incentives to unionized businesses. Unions can enhance representation and voice security in the workplace. This mechanism will also facilitate immigrants making their voice heard and representation secured in the workplace.

- Remove the six-months' restriction for complaints and extend it to at least two years. If the current government truly aspires to protect workers' rights, a two-year limitation will enhance income security for recent immigrants. Extending the complaint period is one of the key mechanisms to reduce abuse of workers' rights and to encourage workers to file a complaint when rights are violated.

- Make culturally appropriate orientation in terms of rights, duties, and safety a requirement on the first day of work. To implement this, the employers may be innovative and still follow the ESA. BC's economy reflects diverse cultural groups' contributions to the labour market. They deserve to have representation and voice security.

- Institute an independent body to review the ESA. Make the Act protect vulnerable workers, including recent immigrants. An independent review will remind the government about the ESA's shortcomings and help improve it, protecting workers' rights and basic security.

- Set up a hotline for the Employment Standards Branch. Staff the hotline with actual people (i.e., avoid a touch-tone phone system) who can answer enquiries in more than one language.

- Set up more Employment Standards Branch offices. Branch offices would be able to clarify clauses of the Act that many immigrants are unaware of.

- Support community organizations and their advocacy work. Community organizations can effectively and inexpensively inform immigrants about their workplace rights.

- Assure housing for recent immigrant workers. This provision would allow for a transition periods, to lay the groundwork for future economic security.

- Provide workers with a subsidized bus pass. This will not only enhance workers' basic security but also reduce pollution, thus advancing the BC government's current environmental agenda. A proportionate discount could be based on income.

The PAR model has been successful in terms of generating alternative policies to counter the BC government's neo-liberal agenda, which shifted responsibilities from the employers to the employees. A highlight of the workshop was that it put an emphasis on advocacy and the role of the community, which should be supported and strengthened through funding and expanded consultation. A stronger role for the community is also a way to facilitate immigrants' settlement and integration quickly. Further, the monitoring and enforcement of the ESA was urged and strengthening of legislation was emphasized.

Summary

Through stories of individual agency, this chapter demonstrated a range of strategies Asian immigrant women utilize after migrating to Canada. It is clear that the road to basic security is an individualized and disjointed path. Those who had well-established family members achieved economic security with minimal difficulties, and their path to basic security was smoother; consequently these immigrants overlooked how racism and sexism are embedded in the labour market. The myth of "hard work" as an ideology, suggesting that hard work will necessarily pave the way to economic security, is pervasive among Asian immigrants, and this neo-liberal approach hinders solidarity and collective resistance strategies among Asian immigrants. However, a consensus is that lack of voice and representation in the workplace compromises basic security.

The PWC is a classic example of the collective strength of the Filipino immigrant community and has several outreach programs to connect to the wider community. Through publishing its reports, the PWC strives to ensure basic security for all marginalized and racialized workers, especially for domestic workers. A broad-based alliance with grassroots groups strengthens the PWC's solidarity in terms of mobilizing people beyond its own community, irrespective of immigration status, gender, race, class, or country of origin.

As a PAR model, the workshop brought together marginalized and racialized immigrants, grassroots groups, academics, researchers, and representatives from provincial and federal governments. Formulating alternative policies demonstrated that if such opportunities are provided, marginalized and racialized immigrants have the ability to make their voices heard. Although the workshop focused on recent immigrants who immigrated after 2002, i.e., after the restructuring of the ESA was implemented, many of the recommendations are equally applicable to Asian immigrants in general. As has already been noted, the proposal that the "minimum wage be raised to ten dollars" was enacted by the BC government with the wage to reach $10.25 on May 1, 2012.

The concluding chapter illustrates the contributions of the book to a wider audience including academics, researchers, community activists, grassroots groups, labour unions, and immigrants.

Notes

1. The workshop was organized by the Philippine Women Centre (PWC), SFU Women's Studies, and the Canadian Centre for Policy Alternatives (CCPA). For details, see Appendix I. The objective of the workshop was to discuss the preliminary findings of the survey of a research project entitled "Asian Immigrants in BC: What does government restructuring mean for immigrants in the labour market?" This project was funded by a grant from the Social Sciences and Humanities Research Council of Canada (SSHRC) through its Community-University Research Alliance Program. Also, the project received a grant from the Vancouver Foundation, BC, which significantly facilitated the research process.

2. The origin, history, growth, and activities of the PWC have been documented in Zaman and Tubajan (2001).

3. The interviewer used the sociological category of class, and asked Nadia about her "class" in Canada. Interestingly, skilled immigrants mentioned "middle class," and hardly perceived themselves belonging to "working class" although they were concentrated in low-waged, non-standard jobs. Here, a major ideological contradiction has been unfolded by this study. However, domestic workers of the LCP were aware of their marginalized and working-class position.

4. The PWC's press release titled "Fists Raised, Heads High! Kamay Lakas, Taas Noo! Philippine Women Centre of BC Celebrating 20 Years of Filipino Women's Empowerment and Collective Transformation" was sent out on September 2, 2010.

The contact address was: Philippine Women Centre of B.C., pwc@kalayaancentre.net.

5.   Grassroots Women sent a press release entitled "Media Advisory: Local Women to Rally on 100th International Women's Day" on Monday, March 8, 2010.

6.   I have identified the workshop as the participatory action research model (PAR) because the study participants actively participated in formulating alternative policies. However, the entire methodology for this book was not participatory action research, and thus, my discussion on methodology did not claim to use the PAR model. Some researchers make little distinction between participatory research and action research. However, it is evident that feminist researchers do make distinctions between the two (for details, see Kirby, Greaves, and Reid 2006; Maguire 1987).

7.   Marjorie Griffin-Cohen, a professor at SFU and a principal investigator and co-chair of the Economic Security Project, funded by SSHRC-CURA (2004–2009), provided a brief introduction of the project. Seth Klein of CCPA, the principal investigator and co-chair of the Economic Security Project, explained the changes to the ESA.

Chapter 7

Vision for an Alliance Across Race, Gender, Class, Sexual Orientation, Age, Dis/ability, and Country of Origin

Until the 1960s, the blatant racist immigration policies in Canada orchestrated the labour market in racialized and gendered ways. In the seventies, the immigration policies shifted from racist to non-racist approaches. In the twenty-first century, seven of the top ten immigrant-sending countries are Asian. A major demographic shift from non-racialized to racialized populations has occurred in Canada, and, as mentioned in the introduction, two-thirds of the population in major cities such as Vancouver and Toronto will be racialized groups, particularly Asian immigrants, by 2031. This study has shed light on Asian immigrants' "basic security" and has demonstrated through Asian immigrants' oral testimonies and survey responses that their security — work security, job security, employment security, etc. — has been compromised in multi-dimensional ways.

As mentioned in the introduction, the *Immigration and Refugee Protection Act* 2002 introduced major changes with the result that skilled, independent immigrants irrespective of race, gender, and country of origin have been attracted to Canada, and Asia has become a major source of immigrants. Through the survey discussed in Chapter Three and individual participants' narratives discussed in Chapters Four and Five, this study has demonstrated that the majority of Asian immigrants are eventually concentrated in low-wage, non-standard, and part-time jobs, which have historically been allocated to racialized immigrants in Canada. The restructuring of the *Employment Standards Act* in BC due to neo-liberal policies has made work more precarious and working conditions less monitored. Working at two jobs simultaneously and job-hopping have become alternative strategies to cope with this situation, as illustrated in Chapters Four and Five.

The study has also demonstrated that despite the current focus on the skilled category, Asian immigrants are marginalized in the labour market because their skills are not recognized in Canada, and the restructuring of the ESA has made permanent, full-time work with access to benefits a difficult goal to achieve.

Indeed, many skilled immigrants have been transformed into what the study has identified as over-skilled proletarians. Further, the mobility in the labour market indicates that many domestic workers moved from "pushing a stroller" to "pushing a wheelchair" — i.e., from child care to elder care — and a few Asian male immigrants moved from janitorial services to working as security guards. It is also evident that the processes and structures of skilled immigrants' erosion of skills are very different from the way in which domestic workers experience erosion of skills, and thus the nature and extent of economic insecurity may be different. It is evident that immigrants under the skilled category are hesitant to be part of a broad-based alliance with various grassroots and social activists' groups, and Asian immigrants' individual voices illustrated this point in Chapter Six. However, the Philippine Women Centre (PWC) — an organization established due to domestic workers' needs — has demonstrated its collective agency while advancing its own agenda (workers' rights in the workplace) by building an alliance and solidarity with a number of grassroots and social activists groups.

Using the International Labour Organization's comprehensive concept of economic security, this study has illustrated how Asian immigrants in BC perform in the labour market and the extent of economic insecurity they encounter in their settlement and integration. Although the ILO's concept overlooks race, sexual orientation, transgender issues, age, and disability and is mostly applicable to able-bodied, young, and heterosexual people, it is generally helpful for exploring any workplace in any country where labour unions and regulations pertinent to labour rights exist. For example, this framework is applicable in India as well as in Canada, but is not applicable in Bangladesh or in Pakistan, where labour unions are almost non-existent. More specifically, this robust framework is suitable for testing the strengths and weaknesses of welfare states in the Northern Hemisphere, where social, liberal, and conservative welfare states exist. Through the ILO's framework, this study has tested the liberal welfare state of Canada and has focused on one province, BC, where neo-liberal policies have resulted in the ESA being restructured. The study has demonstrated that this restructuring has pushed the already vulnerable — recent immigrants, women, and racialized populations — into deregulated work, where the enforcement of the provincial government's ESA and Occupational Health and Safety Regulations are relaxed and has consequently marginalized them further in terms of basic security. The current trend is towards individualization and self-reliance in the workplace, and this individualization reflects the triumph of neo-liberal policy in that the provincial government has reduced the size and power of the Employment Standards Branch and cut back the number of prevention officers at the Workers Compensation Board inspecting workplaces — 192 full-time equivalent safety and hygiene inspectors in 2001 were reduced to 138 by 2004 (Compensation Employees Union 2005). Through the participants' narrations in Chapters Four and Five, it is evident that the changes have strengthened one group of people who are privileged and powerful, i.e., the employers. This illustrates the metaphor of "two Canadas," in which one group is privileged and powerful, and the restructuring of the ESA has further strengthened their position as well as solidified this group. The other group in this study, Asian immigrants, who are a vulnerable population, has become more marginalized and has been forced to work in deregulated workplaces where monitoring and enforcement are relaxed.

The survey discussed in Chapter Three demonstrated that a racialized and gendered space has been produced and reproduced for the domestic workers who migrated under the Live-in Caregiver Program. Thus, they move from child care to care aides and dietary aides, and this change reveals that while they no longer have to live with their employers, low-waged, flexible, temporary, non-standard jobs have become the standard in their lives. In terms of residence, many former domestic workers live in Vancouver's Downtown Eastside, generally populated by marginalized people. Residence in this area has solidified a marginalized living space for many Asian immigrants.

The participants' narratives in Chapters Four and Five uncovered various dimensions of insecurity. They were revealed through the use of the ILO's concept of economic security, demonstrating the utility of this robust concept. Despite all sorts of insecurity, the participants reminded role and significance of the labour unions in the workplace and in their work lives. This study also demonstrated that many Asian immigrants lack knowledge of the ESA because it is no longer posted in the workplace. Through the individual and focus group interviews, which provided information and questions, and the workshop that generated alternative policies, this study raised the consciousness of Asian immigrants about workplace rights. The workshop participants, who included study participants, were enthusiastically engaged in developing alternative policies.

Chapter Five pointed out that the participants preferred to quit exploitative and hazardous jobs rather than complaining and using the "Self-Help Kit," which is a clumsy and lengthy document. Quitting jobs is one of the mechanisms to cope with work insecurity and workplace hazards. The economic boom in BC made quitting jobs feasible; otherwise, many Asian immigrants would have lived indefinitely with workplace hazards, and this would have made them more marginalized and exploited. When economic boom turns into economic recession or slows down due to the current worldwide economic turmoil, hazardous workplaces and economic insecurity are likely to be more pervasive among Asian immigrants.

Reporting on individual and collective agencies in Chapter Six, this study has pointed out that Asian immigrants come from diverse groups and are not homogenous. The ideology of hard work is pervasive among some Asian participants. However, they recognize the absence of voice and representation security, indicating their consciousness about their precarious situation and their basic insecurity. It is clear that the representation of Asian immigrants' voices at various levels would pave the way for the better integration and settlement in Canada, which the federal government strongly emphasizes.

One of the major contributions of this study is that it demonstrates that given opportunities, Asian immigrants who live on the verge of society can make their voices heard by proposing alternative policies, as was discussed in Chapter Six and in Appendix 2. The appendix and the chapter are learning tools for students, academics, and researchers who aspire to organize workshops pertinent to policies for social transformation. Also, the ILO's concept is applicable to any group in the labour force based on country of origin, race, sexual orientation, age, dis/ability, and religion, and any future researcher can utilize this concept.

Afterword

One of the major recommendations of the workshop was to raise the minimum wage and scrap the training wage. In 2010, the Trade Union Research Bureau in BC initiated a collaborative policy research project entitled "BC Employment Standards for the Next Decade" and formed a group named the Employment Standards Advocates Coalition. This group has built a broad-based alliance with cross-sections of organizations including the PWC, BC Federation of Labour, Living Wage Campaign, West Coast Domestic Workers Association, Canadian Centre for Policy Alternatives, CCPA Academic Research Associations, Justice 4 Migrant Workers, and West Coast Leaf. The goal of this Coalition was to launch a public campaign for fundamental changes to the ESA so that it serves the interests of workers and gives them voice — a major issue that the study participants also pointed out. The group recommended an increase in BC's general minimum wage, which was the lowest in Canada and had been frozen for ten years. The Coalition met with officials from the Ministry of Labour in January and February 2011 to express their concerns about the restructuring of the ESA and, in particular, the major changes including the introduction of the first job/training wage. In March 2011, the provincial government finally announced the increase of the minimum wage in three phases over the next year and eliminated the first-job/training wage.

Appendix 1: Asian Immigrants in BC Workshop

**What Does Government Restructuring Mean
for Immigrants in the Labour Market?**
SFU Harbour Centre — April 8, 2006

AGENDA

Context

10:00 am — 10:30 am	Economic Security Project Changes to the Employment Standards Act; defining Economic Security for immigrants

Research Presentation

10:30 am — 11:30 am	Research Methodology Presentation Ethics Challenges Job diversity Participatory Action Research Survey Presentation
11:30 am — 12:30 am	Research Findings Feedback, questions & comments from participants
12:30 pm — 1:30 pm	LUNCH

Alternatives and Policy Changes That Would Enhance Economic Security

1:30 pm — 1:45 pm	Policy Ideas from Surveys
1:45 pm — 3:00 pm	Small Group Discussions (6 groups) Policy changes that would make a difference for Asian immigrants in the labour market and contribute to Economic Security Formulating recommendations for community organizations, municipal, provincial and federal governments and policy planners.
3:00 pm — 3:15 pm	Break
3:15 pm — 4:30 pm	Report Back on Group Discussions Closing Remarks

Appendix 2: Discussion Questions for Participants

Workshop, April 8, 2006
Discussion Questions for Participants
We would like to know your ideas about how to improve economic security in BC, especially for recent immigrants. Please share your thoughts regarding the following discussion questions. Try to focus on ideas for policy alternatives and programs, i.e., changes to policies that could be made or programs that could be designed to improve economic security of recent Asian immigrants. When trying to answer the questions, think, "What could be done that would give me or people I know more economic security?" Try to be as expansive and specific as possible. If you have other questions or topics you would like to address, please feel free to do so.

A) Working Conditions
   1) There are many workplaces with poor working conditions. For example, some workplaces expose their workers to health hazards like chemicals, cleaners, or heavy machinery and tools. Other workplaces expose workers to racial or sexual discrimination. This can have a negative impact on health and well-being. What can be done by the government, unions, employers and/or employees to improve the safety of the workplace environment?

B) Knowledge of Workers' Rights and the *Employment Standards Act*
   1) Some workers are not aware of their rights in the workplace. This may be in regards to WorkSafe BC regulations and acts, the *Employment Standards Act*, or other labour policies. What can be done by the government, unions, employers and/or employees to improve the knowledge of workers' rights in the workplace? Specifically, how can recent immigrants' knowledge of their rights be improved?
   2) In 2002, the BC Liberal government removed the requirement for employers to have a workers' rights poster in the workplace. Do you think workers' rights posters in the workplace would improve workers' knowledge of their rights?

C) Unions
   1) Do you think increasing and expanding unionization will help to improve workers' economic security? If so, what could governments, unions, employers and/or employees do to expand unionization?

D) Training in the Workplace
   1) Some employees do not receive training when they first start a new

job, which can compromise their safety and increase work-related stress. In other workplaces, there are no opportunities for training or advancement of skills. How can the government, unions, employers and/or employees ensure that workers are adequately trained for the jobs they do? What can these same groups do to improve opportunities for training that give workers new skills?

2) Does the "training wage" (six dollars an hour for the first 500 hours of paid employment) improve opportunities for training? Should it be maintained, modified, or scrapped?

E) Complaints in the Workplace

1) Some workers do not feel comfortable complaining to their employer about workplace safety, wages, hours, benefits, or other issues. Some workers feel that complaining might compromise their job security or expose them to abuse. What can be done by governments, unions, employers and/or employees to ensure that workers feel comfortable complaining to their employer about their working conditions?

2) Sometimes, workers' rights violations occur in the workplace. These violations should be reported to the Employment Standards Branch. If no violations are reported, then the Branch cannot investigate a workplace. What can the government, unions, employers and/or employees do to encourage workers to voice their concerns to the Employment Standards Branch?

3) In 2002, the BC Liberal government introduced a new "Self-Help Kit," which must be used by employees before they can make a formal complaint about the workplace to the Employment Standards Branch (with regards to all complaints except those pertaining to children, employee harassment, multiple complaints, farm workers, textile or garment workers, or domestics, and if the company is insolvent). If they do not use the kit, a complaint cannot be filed. This kit is to be used by employers and employees to try to resolve their issues without the intervention of the Branch. Do you think that the kit is a good mechanism for encouraging workers to voice their complaints, and if not, how can it be improved? Should it be scrapped?

4) What can be done to ensure that workers' rights are not violated by employers in the first place?

F) Wages and Compensation

1) What are your thoughts on the minimum wage? Should it be raised?

2) What can be done by the government, unions, employers and/or employees to ensure that workers are fairly compensated for the work they perform?

G) Transportation
  1) All workers need to get themselves to and from work. Many recent immigrants rely heavily on public transportation. How can their access to public transportation be improved by the government, unions, employers and/or employees?

H) Housing
  1) What can be done to improve the housing conditions and costs for recent immigrants?

I) Work Hours
  1) Sometimes workers can get only a part-time job when they would rather have a full-time job. Often, workers must work two part-time jobs. What can be done to ensure that there are enough full-time jobs for workers that want them?
  2) Some workers have only casual jobs, which means their work hours vary from week to week. This can impact economic security since it means that there is uncertainty about what their net monthly income will be. Are there ways to encourage employers to hire more regular workers?

J) Child care
  1) What programs and policies would improve access to child care?

References

Agnew, Vijay (ed.). 2009. *Racialized Migrant Women in Canada*. Toronto: Toronto University Press.

Arat-Koç, Sedef. 1999/2000. "Neo-liberalism, State Restructuring and Immigration: Changes in Canadian Policies in the 1990s." *Journal of Canadian Studies* 34, 2.

Bakan, Abigail B., and Daiva Stasiulis (eds.). 1997. *Not One of the Family: Foreign Domestic Workers in Canada*. Toronto: University of Toronto Press.

____. 1994. "Foreign Domestic Worker Policy in Canada and the Social Boundaries of Modern Citizenship." *Science and Society* 58, 1.

Basok, Tanya. 2003. *Tortillas and Tomatoes: Transmigrant Mexican Harvesters in Canada*. Montreal: McGill-Queen's University Press.

Black, Richard. 2003. "Soaring Remittances Raise New Issues." Migration Policy Institute. At <migrationinformation.org/Feature/display.cfm?ID=127> June.

Blaikie, Heenan. 2002. "Changes to the B.C. Workers Compensation Act Labour & Employment." May 13. At <heenanblaikie.com/en/publications/item;jsessionid...?id=34>.

Boyd, Monica, and Jessica Yiu. 2009. "Immigrant Women and Earnings Inequality in Canada." In Vijay Agnew (ed.), *Racialized Migrant Women in Canada: Essays on Health, Violence, and Equity*. Toronto: University of Toronto Press.

Bramham, Daphne. 2010. "One City's Road to Racial Reconciliation." *Vancouver Sun*, April 3.

Calliste, Agnes, and George Dei (eds.). 2000. *Anti-Racist Feminism: Critical Race and Gender Studies*. Halifax: Fernwood Publishing.

Canada. Citizenship and Immigration. 2011. "Processing Live-in Care-givers in Canada." At <cic.gc.ca/English/resources/manuals/ip/ip04-eng.pdf>.

____. 2005a. "The Live-in Caregiver Program." At <cic.gc.ca/english/pub/caregiver/caregiver-1.html>.

____. 2005b. "Notes for an Address by the Honourable Joe Volpe, Minister of Citizenship and Immigration." At <cic.gc.ca/English/press/speech-volpe/bedget2005.html>.

____. 2004a. *The Monitor*. Fall. At <cic.gc.ca/English/monitor/issue07/02-immigrants.html>.

____. 2004b. *The Monitor*. Spring. At <cic.gc.ca/english/monitor/issue05/02-immigrants.html>.

Canada. Department of Justice. 1995. *Employment Equity Act*. At <laws-lois.justice.gc.ca/eng/acts/E-5.401/page-1.html>.

Canadian Diversity. 2008. "The Experiences of Second Generation Canadians." Spring.

Canadian Issues. 2008. "Immigration and Diversity in Francophone Minority Community." Spring.

____. 2005. "Newcomers, Minorities and Political Participation in Canada." Spring.

_____. 2003. "Immigration: Opportunities and Challenges." April.

Canadian Labour Congress. 2005. "Labour Standards for the 21st Century."

Carrillo, Maria Lourdes. 2009. "Socially Transformative Transnational Feminism: Filipino Women Activists at Home and Abroad." Unpublished dissertation, University of British Columbia, Vancouver.

Cernetig, Miro. 2010. "Immigration Wave Changes Canada's Looks and Sounds." *Vancouver Sun*, March 10.

Choudry, Aziz, Jill Hanley, Stever Jordan, Eric Shragge, and Martha Stiegman. 2009. *Fight Back: Workplace Justice for Immigrants*. Halifax: Fernwood Publishing.

Cohen, Marcy, Arlene McLaren, Zena Sharman, Stuart Murray, Marilee Hughes, and Alec Ostry. 2006. *From Support to Isolation*. Vancouver: Canadian Centre for Policy Alternatives–BC.

Compensation Employees Union. 2005. "WCB Cuts Hurt — Changes at the WCB." At <ceu.bc.ca/files/wcbbrochureweb_format.pdf>.

Das Gupta, Tania. 2009. *Real Nurses and Others: Racism in Nursing*. Halifax: Fernwood Publishing.

Diocson, Cecilia, and the Philippine Women Centre of BC. 2005. "Enhancing Capability and Visibility: Filipinas in Public Policy Engagement." Vancouver: Philippine Women Centre of BC.

Dossa, Parin. 2009. *Racialized Bodies, Disabling Worlds*. Toronto: University of Toronto Press.

Egger, Philippe, and Werner Sengenberger, in collaboration with Peter Auer, Marco Simoni and Conrinne Vargha (eds.). 2003. *Decent Work in Denmark: Employment, Social Efficiency and Economic Security*. Geneva: International Labour Office.

England, Kim, and Bernadette Stiell. 1997. "They Think You're as Stupid as Your English Is: Constructive Foreign Domestic Workers in Toronto." *Environment and Planning* 29.

Esping-Anderson, Gosta. 1990. *The Three Worlds of Welfare Capitalism*. Cambridge: Polity Press.

Fairey, David. 2005. *Eroding Worker Protections: British Columbia's New "Flexible" Employment Standards*. Vancouver: Canadian Centre for Policy Alternatives–BC.

_____. 2002. "No Need to Subsidize Business by Rolling Back Labour Rights." Vancouver: Canadian Centre for Policy Alternatives–BC. At <policyalternatives.ca>.

Friesen, Joe. 2010. "The Changing Face of Canada: As Minority Population Booms, A Visible Majority Emerges." *Globe and Mail*, March 10.

Fudge, Derek. 2005. "Canadian Workers' Rights Assaulted: Collective Bargaining More an Illusion Than a Right." Vancouver: Canadian Centre for Policy Alternatives–BC. At <policyalternatives.ca>.

Fuller, Sylvia. 2004. "Women's Employment in BC: Effects of Government Downsizing and Employment Policy Changes 2001–2004." Vancouver: Canadian Centre for Policy Alternatives–BC. At <policyalternatives.ca>.

Ghai, Dharam (ed.). 2006. *Decent Work: Objectives and Strategies*. Geneva: International Institute of Labour Studies.

Giles, Wenona, and Sedef Arat-Koç (eds.). 1994. *Maid in the Market: Women's Paid Domestic Labour*. Halifax: Fernwood Publishing.

Globe and Mail. 2010. "Concentration of Growth in Cities Could Give Rise to 'Two Canadas.'" March 10.

_____. 2006. "Immigration Target Hits 25-year High." November 1.

Grant, H., and A. Sweetman. 2004. "Introduction to Economic and Urban Issues in Canadian

Immigration Policy." *Canadian Journal of Urban Research* 13.

Gupta, Tania Das. 2009. *Real Nurses and Others: Racism in Nursing*. Halifax: Fernwood Publishing.

Habib, Sanzida Z. 2003. "Gender, Race and Class Biases in Canadian Immigration Policies: The Impact on Women of Color." Unpublished MA extended essay, Simon Fraser University, Vancouver.

Halli, Shiva S., and Leo Driedger. 1999. *Immigrant Canada: Demographic, Economic, and Social Challenges*. Toronto: University of Toronto Press.

Infometrica Limited. 2001. *Canada's Recent Immigrants: A Comparative Portrait Based on the 1996 Census*. Citizenship and Immigration Canada.

International Labour Organization. 2004. *Economic Security for a Better World*. Geneva: International Labour Office.

Irwin, John, Stephen McBride, and Tanya Strubin. 2005. *Child and Youth Employment Standards: The Experience of Young Workers Under British Columbia's New Policy Regime*. Vancouver: Canadian Centre for Policy Alternatives–BC.

Jakubowski, Lisa Marie. 1997. *Immigration and Legalization of Racism*. Halifax: Fernwood Publishing.

Kelly, Philip. 2006. "Filipina/os in Canada: Economic Dimensions of Immigration and Settlement." Working Paper #48. Toronto: Joint Center of Excellence for Research on Immigration and Settlement.

Kirby, Sandra, Lorraine Greaves, and Colleen Reid. 2006. *Experience Research Social Change: Methods Beyond the Mainstream* (second edition). Peterborough, ON: Broadview Press.

Klein, Seth. 2002. "No Evidence to Justify Lowering the Floor: A Submission to the BC Employment Standards Review." Vancouver: Canadian Centre for Policy Alternatives–BC. At <policyalternatives.ca> January 3.

Kofman, Eleonore, and Parvati Raghuram. 2005. "Gender and Skilled Bigrants: Into and Beyond the Work Place." *Geoforum* 36, 2 (March).

Lerner, Sally, Charles Clark, and Robert Needham. 1999. *Basic Income: Economic Security for All Canadians*. Toronto: Between the Lines.

Li, Peter S. 2003. *Destination Canada: Immigration Debates and Issues*. Oxford: Oxford University Press.

____. 2001. "The Market Worth of Immigrants' Educational Credentials." *Canadian Public Policy* 27, 1.

Maaka, Roger C.A., and Chris Andersen. 2006. *The Indigenous Experience: Global Perspectives*. Toronto: Canadian Scholars' Press.

MacDonald, Diane. 2002. "More Labour Code Amendments Invite Increased Confrontation." Vancouver: Canadian Centre for Policy Alternatives–BC. At <policyalternatives.ca> April 1.

Maguire, Patricia. 1987. *Doing Participatory Research: A Feminist Approach*. Amherst: University of Massachusetts.

Massey, Douglas, et al. 1993. "Theories of International Migration: A Review and Appraisal." *Population and Development Review* 19, 1.

Meyers, Eytan. 2000. "Theories of International Immigration Policy: A Comparative Analysis." *International Migration Review* 34, 4.

Migration Policy Institute. 2005. "Remittance Data." At <migrationinformation.org/USfocus/print.cfm?ID=137>.

Mohanty, Chandra Talpade. 1991. "Introduction." In Chandra Talpade Mohanty, Ann

Russo, and Lourdes Torres (eds.), *Third World Women and the Politics of Feminism.* Bloomington: Indiana University Press.

Moore, Graeme. 2004. "Hand-Harvesters of Fraser Valley Berry Crops: New Era Protection of Vulnerable Employees." Vancouver: BC Federation of Labour.

New Westminster City. 2009. "Reconciliation Research Findings: Council Records." At <newwestcity.ca/business/planning_development/social_planning/articles215.php>.

O'Neil, Kevin. 2004. "Labour Export as Government Policy: The Case of the Philippines," *Migration Policy Source.* At <migrationinformation.org/Feature/print.cfm?ID=191>.

Oreopoulos, Philip. 2009. "Employers Discriminate Against Applicants with Non-English Names," Metropolis BC Working Papers, May, Vancouver: Metropolis BC.

Philippine Women Centre of BC. 2000. *The New Frontier for Filipino Mail-Order Brides.* Ottawa: Status of Women Canada.

____. 1997. *"Trapped: Holding on to the Knife's Edge: Economic Violence Against Filipino Migrant/Immigrant Women."* Vancouver: Philippine Women Centre of BC.

____. 1996. *Housing Needs Assessment of Filipino Domestic Workers.* Vancouver: Philippine Women Centre of BC.

Picot, G. 2004. "The Deteriorating Economic Welfare of Canadian Immigrants." *Canadian Journal of Urban Research* 13.

Pratt, Geraldine. 2004. *Working Feminism.* Philadelphia: Temple University Press.

____. 1999. "Is This Really Canada? Domestic Workers' Experiences in Vancouver, BC." In Janet Henshall Momsen (ed.), *Gender, Migration and Domestic Service.* London and New York: Routledge.

Pratt, Geraldine, in collaboration with the Philippine Women Centre of BC. 2003. "From Migrant to Immigrant: Domestic Workers Settle in Vancouver, Canada." Research on Immigration and Integration in the Metropolis. November. Vancouver.

Razack, Sherene H. (ed.). 2002. *Race, Space, and the Law: Unmapping a White Settler Society.* Toronto: Between the Lines.

Reitz, Jeffery. 2001. "Immigrant Skill Utilization in the Canadian Labour Market: Implications of Human Capital Research." At <utoronto.ca/ethnicstudies/reitz.html>.

Schiller, Nina Glick, and Linda Basch. 1995. "From Immigrant to Transmigrant: Theorizing Transnational Migration." *Anthropological Quarterly* 68, 1.

Scholefield, Ethelbert, and Fredric Howay. 1914. *British Columbia from the Earliest Times to the Present. Vol 2.* Vancouver: S.J. Clarke.

Sharma, Nandita. 2001. "On Being Not Canadian: The Social Organization of 'Migrant Workers' in Canada." *Canadian Review of Sociology and Anthropology* 38, 4.

Simmons, Alan. 1990. "'New Wave' Immigrants: Origins and Characteristics." In Shiva Halli, Trovato and Leo Driedger (eds.), *Ethnic Demography: Canadian Immigrant, Race and Cultural Variation.* Kingston: McGill-Queens University.

Standing, Guy (ed.). 2004. *Promoting Income Security as a Right.* London: Anthem Press.

____. 2004. "About Time: Basic Income Security as a Right." In Guy Standing (ed.), *Promoting Income Security as a Right.* London: Anthem Press.

Stasiulis, Daiva, and Abigail Bakan. 2005. *Migrant Women in Canada and the Global System.* Toronto: University of Toronto.

Stinson, Jane, Nancy Pollak, and Marcy Cohen. 2005. *The Pains of Privatization: How Contracting Out Hurts Health Support Workers, Their Families, and Health Care.* Vancouver: Canadian Centre for Policy Alternatives–BC.

Taylor, K.W. 1991. "Racism in Canadian Immigration Policy." *Canadian Ethnic Studies* 23, 1.

Thobani, Sunera. 2007. *Exalted Subjects: Studies in the Making of Race and Nation in Canada.* Toronto: University of Toronto.

____. 1999. "Sponsoring Immigrant Women's Inequalities." *Canadian Woman Studies* 23, 2.

Tremblay, Diane-Gabrielle. 2009. "Work, Insecurity, and Social Justice." *Studies in Social Justice* 3, 2

Vancouver Sun. 2010. "Vancouver's Emerging New Face." March 10.

Vosko, Leah (ed.). 2006. *Precarious Employment: Understanding Labour Market Insecurity in Canada.* Montreal & Kingston: McGill-Queens University Press.

Walker, Barrington (ed.). 2008. *The History of Immigration and Racism in Canada: Essential Readings.* Toronto: Canadian Scholars' Press.

Wallace, Bruce, Seth Klein, and Marge Reitsma-Street. 2006. *Denied Assistance: Closing the Front Door on Welfare in BC.* Vancouver: Canadian Centre for Policy Alternatives–BC.

Warburton, Rennie. 1999. "The Workingmen's Protective Association, Victoria, BC, 1878: Racism, Intersectionality and Status Politics." *Labour/Le Travail* 43 (Spring).

WorkSafeBC. 2012. "Changes to OHS Regulations: Policy Updates for 2003 & 2002. At <http://www2.worksafebc.com/Publications/OHSRegulation/changestoohsregulation.asp?ReportID=33088>.

Zaman, Habiba. 2006. *Breaking the Iron Wall: Decommodification and Immigrant Women's Labor in Canada.* Lanham: Lexington Books.

____. 2004. "Transnational Migration and the Commodification of Im/migrant Female Labourers in Canada." *International Journal of Canadian Studies* 29.

Zaman, Habiba, Cecilia Diocson, and Rebecca Scott. 2007. *Workplace Rights for Immigrants in BC: The Case of Filipino Workers.* Vancouver: Canadian Centre for Policy Alternatives–BC.

Zaman, Habiba, and Gina Tubajon. 2001. "'Globalization from Below': Feminization of Migration, Resistance and Empowerment — A Case Study." *Canadian Journal of Development Studies* 22.